HERITAGE OF THE SAINTS

HERITAGE OF THE SAINTS

HERBERT LOCKYER

WHITAKER HOUSE

Unless otherwise indicated, all Scripture quotations are taken from the King James Version of the Holy Bible. Scripture quotations marked (RSV) are taken from Revised Standard Version of the Bible, copyright © 1946, 1952, and 1971 by the Division of Christian Education of the National Council of the Churches of Christ in the United States of America. Used by permission. All rights reserved. Scripture quotations marked (RV) are taken from the Revised Version of the Holy Bible. The Scripture quotation translated by Weymouth is taken from *The New Testament in Modern Speech: An Idiomatic Translation into Everyday English from the Text of "The Resultant Greek Testament"* by R. F. (Richard Francis) Weymouth.

THE HERITAGE OF THE SAINTS:
STUDIES IN THE HOLY SPIRIT

ISBN: 978-1-62911-564-1
eBook ISBN: 978-1-62911-586-3
Printed in the United States of America

Whitaker House
1030 Hunt Valley Circle
New Kensington, PA 15068
www.whitakerhouse.com

Library of Congress Cataloging-in-Publication Data

Names: Lockyer, Herbert, author.
Title: The heritage of the saints / Herbert Lockyer.
Other titles: Heritage of saints, or, studies in the Holy Spirit
Description: New Kensington, PA : Whitaker House, 2016. | Originally published under title: The heritage of saints, or, studies in the Holy Spirit : London : Pickering & Inglis, 1936.
Identifiers: LCCN 2015043766 | ISBN 9781629115641 (trade pbk. : alk. paper)
Subjects: LCSH: Holy Spirit.
Classification: LCC BT121.3 .L63 2016 | DDC 231/.3--dc23 LC record available at http://lccn.loc.gov/2015043766

1 2 3 4 5 6 7 8 9 10 11 23 22 21 20 19 18 17 16

CONTENTS

Preface 7

1. The Holy Spirit Himself 9
2. The Holy Spirit in the Believer 25
3. The Holy Spirit in the Life of the Lord Jesus 39
4. The Holy Spirit and Service 53
5. Sufferings of the Holy Spirit 67
6. Sevenfold Manifestation of the Holy Spirit 81
7. The Holy Spirit as Fire 97
8. The Holy Spirit in 2 Corinthians 3 109

About the Author 123

PREFACE

Years ago, when requested to give a message or two at a conference upon the topic of the Holy Spirit, I discovered my lack of any consecutive ideas of the theme appointed.

Accordingly, as soon as the conference was over, I gave myself up to the task of obtaining a thorough understanding of the truth revealed in the Scriptures concerning the Spirit. After months of prayerful meditation, I was able to classify and present an outline of what the Word of God had to say about the Spirit of God.

Someday I hope to print the results of such a blessed study. Meantime, owing to an incessant demand for their issue, I have collected several of the lectures on the Holy Spirit, which the Lord has been pleased to use both in Britain and America.

These addresses were delivered at the Moody Ministerial Conference, Montrose, Pennsylvania, where they were transcribed and are, with slight alteration, given as spoken. Such a form explains certain phrases and references.

May the life-giving Spirit use them in printed form, even as He blessed them when orally presented.

—Herbert Lockyer

CHAPTER ONE:

THE HOLY SPIRIT HIMSELF

It is essential to understand the truth regarding the person and work of the Spirit of God as unfolded in the Scriptures. Many people seem to think it is not necessary to have a clear conception of the truth of the Spirit because, they say, "The Spirit Himself believes in self-effacement; He never speaks about Himself." Then they proceed to quote John 16:13: *"He shall not speak of himself."* Because He does not speak of Himself, they claim, there is no need for us to say much about Him. But the little word *"of"* in that verse actually means *from,* which gives you a different understanding of the passage altogether. The word that fell from the lips of our Lord does not teach the self-effacement of the Holy Spirit but implies that the divine Spirit did not originate the truth He proclaimed, "He shall not speak *from* Himself." The revelation He gives was received, not self-conceived. The presence and power of the Spirit is an essential part of divine revelation. Believing as we do that the Holy Spirit made possible the Bible, we know that the Spirit of God has a great deal to say about Himself, for the Bible is full of the truth of the Spirit. You cannot understand many parts of the Word of God unless you fully accept the truth regarding the personality of the Spirit, for spiritual things are spiritually discerned.

Then in the next place, we should study the truth of the Spirit, seeing that the Spirit is the direct Agent between our hearts and the Lord, in this dispensation. In the Old Testament, you have the age of God the Father; in the Gospels, the age of God the Son; and from the Acts to Revelation, the age of God the Holy Spirit; and we live in the dispensation of the grace of God, when the Holy Spirit is functioning as the direct Agent between the hearts of the believers and the Lord Jesus Christ.

Again, we should know the truth of the Spirit, for is He not the administrator of the affairs of the church? It was He, on the day of Pentecost, who brought the church into being; He was responsible for her inception. The church, therefore, has intimate association with the Spirit of God. He is indeed within the church, administering all her affairs, and the church is only vital and powerful as she recognizes the lordship of the Spirit.

It is the purpose of the devil to prevent men and women from knowing the full truth regarding the personality and the power and the purpose of the Holy Spirit. Satan is an evil spirit, and he strives in every possible way to keep us from the Holy Spirit; for he knows full well that if the Spirit of God fills and possesses our lives, then his sway will be forever obliterated. When we enjoy the fullness of the Holy Spirit, the reign of the enemy is brought to an end. Nothing can defeat the purpose of the devil in your life and mine like the realization of the truth of the Spirit's indwelling and infilling. Of course, it is very necessary to realize that it is impossible to understand the truth of the Holy Spirit unless we know the Holy Spirit Himself. The more we know the person, the more it will be possible for us to understand His personality and work.

There are three ways by which we can approach our meditation on the Holy Spirit:

I. HE IS NOT AN INFLUENCE

The Holy Spirit is not an influence. Let me stress this aspect of our theme, that the Spirit of God is more than an influence. During the third century, the error crept into the church that the Spirit of God was not a person but only an influence, an emanation from God, some kind of power or energy flowing from Him. And such an error has never left the church. This is the reason why so many, when speaking of the Holy Spirit, refer to Him as "It."

Suppose I came to your home, and you, showing me your son, related to me all his achievements at school, his gifts, and his abilities. After your description of him, suppose I said, "*It* seems to be very clever." How would you feel if I addressed your boy as "It"? Let us not grieve the Holy Spirit by denying His personality; He is not some*thing* but Some*one*, not "It" but a divine person.

Largely as a result of modernistic teaching, men have again come to look upon the third person of the Trinity as a mere influence emanating from God. True, He possesses many influences—"He came, sweet influence to impart" as we so often sing[1]—but He Himself is not an influence, He is a divine person. He is God.

II. HIS PERSONALITY

Let us now face the truth regarding His personality. Believing that He is a person, we must try to prove such a fact from the Word of God.

"THE"

There are one or two terms we must try to understand before we can fully comprehend the biblical revelation of the Spirit. There is the article *the*, and we ought to pay attention to that. In some references, the article is omitted and you have the plain term, *Holy Spirit*. Then again, in many references the article is used, and the simple explanation of the use and omission of the article is this: where you have the article *the*, the personality of the Holy Spirit is in the mind of the writer; but where the article is omitted, it is the power of the Holy Spirit that is stressed by the writer: *"And they were all filled with the Holy Ghost, and began to speak with other tongues, as the Spirit gave them utterance"* (Acts 2:4). And further, *"He said unto them, Have ye received the Holy Ghost since ye believed? And they said unto him, We have not so much as heard whether there be any Holy Ghost"* (Acts 19:2).

"HOLY"

Why is He called "the Holy Spirit?" Because He is holy within Himself; He comes from a holy God, represents a holy Savior in a world most unholy, and because His great work is

---

1. Harriet Auber, "Spirit of the Psalms," 1829.

to fashion men and women into the holiness of God. "Every thought of holiness [is] His alone."[2]

"SPIRIT"

The word *ghost* is the old English term for *spirit,* and *spirit* is used in contrast to that which is of the flesh and material. My spirit is the part of me that acts, and so in the Holy Spirit you have God in action.

THE THIRD PERSON

Then we refer to Him as the third person of the blessed Trinity. He is spoken of in that way, not in any sense of inferiority, for He is co-equal with the Father and with the Son. We speak of Him as the third person because His is the last revealed personality. The Old Testament is full of God; there you have the revelation of the Father. The four gospels are taken up with the Lord Jesus Christ. He came revealing the Father. With the ascension of the Lord Jesus, there came the descent of the Holy Spirit, and now we live in the age of the Spirit when it is His work to reveal the Lord Jesus to us even as the Lord Jesus revealed the Father. Thus He is spoken of as the third person because His is the last revealed personality.

I think the three persons forming the Trinity are illustrated in the root, the stem, and the fruit. In the root imbedded in the ground, you have a fitting type of God the Father; He is the foundation of all things. Out of the Father, the Lord Jesus sprang and is referred to as the "stem" or as the "branch." He came forth from the Father, and then the Holy Spirit appeared as the gift of the ascended Lord and He is the "fruit." Paul refers

---

2. Ibid.

to the "fruit of the Spirit," and in the Spirit of God you have the fruit of the foundational work of the Lord Jesus Christ.

It is very easy to prove the personality of the Holy Spirit of God from the Word of God. For example:

1. The same words are used of the Holy Spirit as of any other person. Our Lord has a great deal to say about the Holy Spirit. Thirteen times in John 16, He refers to the Spirit as "He" and "Him," and because our Lord used the personal pronoun, we know that the Spirit is indeed a person.

2. Language has no meaning if the Spirit of God does not possess personality. The actions performed against the Holy Spirit are absurd if He does not have personality. He can be blasphemed; He can be lied against, tempted, and resisted; and all these actions are utterly impossible unless you have personality. The wind is an influence, but you cannot grieve the wind. Grief is only possible where you have personality. Thus these actions performed by men against the Spirit of God prove His personality.

3. And then the actions performed by Him declare the truth of His personality. The Word declares that the Spirit thinks, plans, speaks, guides, and strives.

4. He also has the true elements of personality. It is difficult for people to believe in His personality seeing He does not possess a body. We can believe in the personality of Christ because He indwelt a human body, and that body glorified is now the center of attraction in glory. Some minds, however, find it hard to comprehend the truth of the Spirit's personality, seeing He does not have a body.

There is a difference between personality and body. I have a personality altogether apart from my person, my body. Suppose death laid hold of me and my body fell to the ground; well, my personality would remain the same. Although my body is the medium through which personality reveals itself, when death attacks the body, the personality within is not influenced by death. We live on; although death may lay hold of our persons or our bodies. My personality is really myself; my soul is myself. And within what we call personality, you have the mind, the heart, and the will. With the mind, we think; with the heart, we love; and with the will, we act or decide. When the body dies, these three possessions still exist, for we carry with us into eternity our minds and our hearts and our wills.

Now, the Holy Spirit, while He does not have a body, does possess the true elements of personality. He has a mind. With our minds, we think; and the Holy Spirit has a mind and is therefore able to think, act, plan, and guide. It was He who made possible the Word of God. Think of the wisdom displayed in the compilation of the Word of God!

Then there is the heart; and with the heart, we love. The heart is the source of affection; and we read, do we not, about the love of the Spirit? At His baptism, you remember how the Lord Jesus received a definite anointing of the Spirit. The Spirit of God came upon our Lord in the form of a dove. Why the dove? Because it is a love bird, and in such you have a type of the loving nature of the Spirit. This is why He is able to shed abroad in our hearts the love of God.

Again there is the will; and with the will, we decide. The mind sees something, the heart loves it, and then the will surrenders to it. Now, the Holy Spirit has a will. Paul speaks not only about the mind of the Spirit and the love of the Spirit, but also in 1 Corinthians 12, where you have outlined the gifts of the Spirit, the apostle tells us that the Spirit bestows His gifts severally as He will. Thus He possesses all the elements contributing to what we call personality.

5. His personality can also be proved from the emblems that are used in the New Testament to describe His operations. Let me refer to two of these emblems. Our Lord spoke of the Holy Spirit as the Advocate. "I will send another Comforter or Advocate." (See John 14:16.) If the Spirit of God is not a person, there is no significance at all in the word that Jesus used to describe the ministry of the Spirit. An advocate pleads our cause; mere influence could never plead such. If I were in difficulty and required aid, would a mere influence help me? Not a bit of it. The Spirit of God, then, is a person because He can act as an Advocate in the time of need.

The Lord also refers to Him as a Porter. In John 10, where He talks about Himself as the Good Shepherd caring for the sheep, He speaks of the Holy Spirit in this descriptive fashion: "*To him the porter openeth*" (John 10:3). The Spirit is a Porter and it is He who opens the door and introduces the seeking sinner to the seeking Savior. Thus in the various titles that are used to describe the ministry of the Spirit, you have a further evidence of His personality.

III. HIS DEITY

In the last place, there is the deity of the Spirit, for He is not only a person, but a divine Person. The Bible does not set out to prove the personality and the deity of the Spirit; it simply states the fact in no uncertain terms. There are one or two ways, however, by which we are assured that the Spirit of God is a divine person:

1. He is associated with the Father and the Son. For example, there is His association with God and Christ in the work of redemption. In Hebrews 9:14, the Father, the Son, and the Spirit are all brought together in the work of the cross: "*Who* [the Lord Jesus Christ] *through the eternal Spirit offered himself without spot to God.*" Here you have the Father, Son, and Spirit related in the work of atonement. In the fifteenth chapter of Luke, you discover three wonderful pictures of the redeeming work of God, and how all the three persons in the Trinity are united in such a blessed work. In the loving father welcoming the prodigal, you have a picture of the heart of God, the heavenly Father. In the shepherd trying to find the lost sheep, you have a glimpse into the tender heart of the Good Shepherd out on the mountainside of sin, seeking the straying sheep. In the woman searching for the lost pieces of silver, you have portrayed the work of the Spirit of God in salvation. So Father, Son, and Spirit are all united in the marvelous work of bringing sinners to the knowledge of redeeming grace.

Further, you have all three related in the baptismal formula in Matthew 28:19–20, the last command of our blessed Lord: "*Go ye, therefore, and teach all nations, baptizing them in the name of the Father, and of the Son, and of the Holy Ghost: teaching them to observe all things whatsoever I have commanded you: and, lo, I am with you always, even unto the end of the world.*"

All three are also brought together in the church's benediction in 2 Corinthians 13:14, "*The grace of the Lord Jesus Christ, and the love of God, and the communion of the Holy Ghost, be with you all.*"

2. In the next place, you discover that the Spirit of God possesses the same attributes as the Father and the Son. Now what are some of these attributes?

DEITY

First of all, there is deity. We know that God is divine and that the Lord Jesus was, and is, divine; and in like manner the Holy Spirit shares the same attribute of deity. In Acts 5:3–5, where the apostle Peter is bringing home to Ananias and Sapphira the fact of their dreadful sin, it is very clear that a comparison of the terms used indicates the faith of the early church in the deity of the Spirit:

> *But Peter said, Ananias, why hath Satan filled thine heart to lie to the Holy Ghost, and to keep back part of the price of the land? Whiles it remained, was it not thine own? and after it was sold, was it not in thine own power? why hast thou conceived this thing in thine heart? thou hast not lied unto men, but unto God. And Ananias hearing these words fell down, and gave up the ghost: and great fear came on all them that heard these things.* (Acts 5:3–5)

OMNIPOTENCE

Omnipotence simply means "all-powerful." We know that God is almighty and that the Lord Jesus in the days of His flesh was mantled with remarkable power. The Holy Spirit in like manner possesses the same attribute. Micah 3:8 says, "*I am full of power by the spirit of the* Lord."

In the last book of the Bible, you have a reference to the seven horns, which are the seven Spirits of God: "*And I beheld, and, lo, in the midst of the throne and of the four beasts, and in the midst of the elders, stood a Lamb as it had been slain, having seven horns and seven eyes, which are the seven Spirits of God sent forth into all the earth*" (Revelation 5:6). The horn is the symbol of power, and in the seven horns—related as they are to the Spirit of God—you have emphasized the thought of His omnipotence. He is all-powerful.

OMNIPRESENCE

Omnipresence means that a person has the power to be everywhere at the same time. In the days of His flesh, the Lord Jesus limited Himself. He indwelt a human body and so could only be in one place at a given time. But then, near the time of his death, He explained to His disciples that *"It is expedient for you that I go away: for if I go not away, the Comforter will not come unto you"* (John 16:7). He went away in order that all disciples, no matter where they might gather themselves together, might realize and enjoy His presence.

Since the day of Pentecost, in the Person of the Holy Spirit, the Lord is everywhere at the same time. *"Whither shall I go from thy spirit? or whither shall I flee from thy presence?"* (Psalm 139:7). Here we are realizing His presence, and yet in almost every other town and city, there are people gathered together in the name of the Lord Jesus. Wherever the saints are to be found, they realize the presence of the Holy Spirit.

OMNISCIENCE

Omniscience means "all knowledge." First Corinthians 2:10–11 says, *"But God hath revealed them unto us by his Spirit: for the Spirit searcheth all things, yea, the deep things of God. For what man knoweth the things of a man, save the spirit of man which is in him? Even so the things of God knoweth no man, but the Spirit of God."*

In the book of Revelation, as previously noted, the phrase, "the seven eyes," is applied to the Spirit of God: *"having seven horns and seven eyes, which are the seven Spirits of God sent forth into all the earth"* (Revelation 5:6). The apostle John, in using this metaphor, implies that the Spirit of God has perfect vision, can see all things, and can discern our intents and judge our motives. Such is a solemnizing thought. To know that nothing is hid from the searching glance and from the perfect knowledge of the Spirit of God ought to lead us to walk humbly before our God.

ETERNITY

Eternity is another attribute of deity. God is eternal, and Christ is eternal. In Hebrews 9:14 we have the phrase, *"the eternal Spirit,"* which means that the Spirit has no revealed beginning and no revealed ending. He is coeternal with the Father and with the Son.

HOLINESS

Holiness is also an attribute of deity. God is holy; Christ is holy; and in like manner, the Spirit is referred to something like one hundred times as "the Holy Spirit." He has this title because His great mission is to lay hold of men and women who are so unholy and transform them into the holiness of God. *"Be ye holy; for I am holy"* (1 Peter 1:16) is God's command, but it is the Holy Spirit who alone can impart divine holiness.

SOVEREIGNTY

As we think of the Spirit of God, we realize that He possesses this attribute as well as the others referred to. Take the teaching of the apostle in 2 Corinthians 3:17, where in the English Revised Version you have this phrase: *"The Lord is that Spirit: and where the Spirit of the Lord is, there is liberty"* (RV).

I think that Joseph B. Rotherham has a very beautiful way of translating it: *"Where the Spirit is Lord, there is liberty"* (Rotherham's Emphasized Bible). He is indeed the Spirit of the Lord; He comes from the Lord; and it is likewise true that where *"the Spirit is Lord, there is liberty."* This is why the early church was so active and powerful; she recognized the lordship of the Spirit. He dominated the church, and within such, everything was referred to the Spirit of God. This is why we should rename "Acts," "The Acts of the Holy Spirit through the Apostles." And not until the church returns to the recognition of the lordship of the Spirit of God can she expect Pentecostal power and results. When we recognize His sovereignty in our individual lives, there is liberty in prayer, in worship, and in service.

3. Last of all, the works performed by the Holy Spirit are only possible to deity. Think of the four outstanding works of the Spirit of God:

There is *creation*. Only God can create, and so the first reference to the Spirit of God is in Genesis 1:2. Right there at the beginning of the Bible, we read that *"the Spirit of God moved upon the face of the waters."* It was He who made possible the beautiful world in which we live. In Job 26:13, we are told, *"By his spirit he hath garnished the heavens."* So the Spirit of God created the world and beautified the heavens. And as He was responsible for creation, He is likewise responsible for our new creation. As He brought beauty and order out of chaos at the beginning, so He wonderfully transforms human lives now.

In the next place, *inspiration* streams from deity. Take what David has to say in 2 Samuel 23:2–3: *"The Spirit of the LORD spake by me, and His word was in my tongue. The God of Israel said, the Rock of Israel spake to me, He that ruleth over men must be just, ruling in the fear of God."* Link this to what the New

Testament has to say about the Spirit, who, as God, has power to inspire. "*For the prophecy came not in old time by the will of man: but holy men of God spake as they were moved by the Holy Ghost*" (2 Peter 1:21). It is He who is responsible for all true inspiration. He inspired men to write the Old Testament and used others to form the New Testament.

Then you have *regeneration*. Who can regenerate except God? God is the Father of Life. The Spirit is referred to as the Spirit of life; and as such, He can regenerate. Coming to the teaching of our Lord in John 3, in His conversation with Nicodemus, He declared that the Holy Spirit is the Author of regeneration. I trust that you have experienced this initial work of the Spirit, that you know what it is to be wrought upon by the Spirit of God and raised from self into that new life that God has for you in His dear Son.

The last work of deity is *resurrection*. God alone is able to raise from the dead, as the apostle teaches in 1 Corinthians 15. The Lord had power to raise from the dead; and the Spirit of God shares the same power. It was He who made possible the resurrection of our Lord Jesus. As He raised Christ from the dead, so, indwelling believers, He is the pledge of their resurrection. We are sealed with the Holy Spirit until the day of redemption.

What a heritage we have in the Holy Spirit! Let us not forget the vast resources placed at our disposal in Him. There is no reason at all for our spiritual impoverishment, for we have a mighty gift indeed in our ascended Lord. It is our solemn obligation to possess our possessions. The Holy Spirit is indeed holy, but alas, we are so sinful. He is all-powerful; we are so weak. He is so wise; we are so ignorant. He is ever present, yet we are ignorant of His nearness. We sometimes act as though

He does not indwell our hearts. He is the sovereign One, but alas, we are so often defeated because we will not recognize and revere His lordship. Before He left His disciples, He declared, *"Ye shall receive power, after that Holy Ghost is come upon you"* (Acts 1:8). As we learn to obey the Holy Spirit and give Him the full control of our lives, we come by a new way altogether to believe in His personality and deity.

CHAPTER TWO:

THE HOLY SPIRIT IN THE BELIEVER

We cannot emphasize too strongly the need of a deeper study and greater apprehension of the truth regarding the personality and work of the Holy Spirit. A growing and accurate knowledge of the truth of the Spirit is vastly important, seeing that He is the direct Agent between our hearts and the Lord. In the goodness of God, we have two mediators: the one between God and man in general is the Man, Christ Jesus; the other between the Lord Jesus and His own is the Holy Spirit. The prevalent weakness and powerlessness so evident today is attributable to a deficient understanding of the resources placed at our disposal in the Holy Spirit. There are three distinct phases of the Spirit's work in connection with the walk and the witness of the believer to be found in John's gospel.

First, His incoming, John 3:5–8. Here our Lord emphasized the truth of regeneration. "*That which is born of the Spirit is spirit*" (John 3:6). Second, His up-springing, John 4:14. Water is one of the outstanding symbols used of the ministry of the Spirit. "*But whosoever drinketh of the water that I shall give him shall never thirst; but the water that I shall give him shall be in him a well of water springing up into everlasting life*" (John 4:14). Third, His outflowing, John 7:37–39. There our Lord indicates the influence of the believer in the world.

> *In the last day, that great day of the feast, Jesus stood and cried, saying, If any man thirst, let him come unto me, and drink. He that believeth on me, as the scripture hath said, out of his belly shall flow rivers of living water. (But this spake he of the Spirit, which they that believe on him should receive: for the Holy Ghost was not yet given; because that Jesus was not yet glorified.)* (John 7:37–39)

In the first reference, the Spirit of God *regenerates*. In the second, He *permeates*. In the third, He *irrigates*. So He flows *in*, flows *through*, and then flows *out*. These three aspects are related to the three great truths wrapped up in our life as believers. In John 3 the Holy Spirit is related to our *salvation*, in John 4 to our *sanctification*, and in John 7, to our *service*.

I. THE NATURE OF HIS THREEFOLD OPERATION

In the first place, let us try to understand all that is involved in the threefold operation of the Spirit of God and of how inspiring it is to appreciate the nature of the Spirit's in-working and out-working! We readily admit that our corporate church life and our personal Christian life would be more fascinating and fruitful if we lived under the sway of the Holy Spirit.

1. HIS INCOMING (JOHN 3:5–8)

"Except a man be born of water and of the Spirit, he cannot enter into the kingdom of God" (John 3:5). Here we have the initial work of the Spirit and, in one sense, His final work; for once the gate of the human spirit is open, the Holy Spirit enters once and for all. As the gift of the ascended Lord, the Holy Spirit came on the day of Pentecost for the express purpose of forming the church, which is His body, and He will be associated with the church until her completion and translation. So, originally and fundamentally, the baptism with the Holy Spirit is that coming of the Holy Spirit whereby the mystical body was instituted. *"By one Spirit are we all baptized into one body"* (1 Corinthians 12:13). And the baptism with the Holy Spirit is equivalent, in our experience, to regeneration. By the work of the Spirit, we are baptized into the body known as the church.

There are some friends who believe in praying for what they call the baptism with the Holy Spirit. But why ask God for something that has already been accomplished by the Lord? I know, of course, that we all ultimately desire the same experience, but it is always fitting to express the desire of our heart in biblical terms. One baptism, many fillings or infillings.

Now, there are two very simple things to remember at this point. In the first place, the Holy Spirit enters to regenerate. As the Spirit of life, He brings about a new order of things, and the work of regeneration is the basis of all further work in the life of the believing sinner. I trust all of us are conscious of this, that we have been regenerated by the Spirit of God. He enters to regenerate. Then He enters to remain. And here we come to emphasize the teaching of our Lord in John 14:16, *"He may abide with you for ever."*

It is very necessary to dwell upon this, seeing that there are some hymns on the Holy Spirit not altogether true to divine revelation. Never take your theology from hymns. We thank God for multitudes of them. They were written by Spirit-inspired men, and they aid us in our worship and devotions. At times, however, we stumble across hymns that are not altogether true to what we have in the Word of God. For example, there is one hymn containing a verse that speaks of our grieving the Holy Spirit away from the heart. That is impossible. We have just read He is to *"abide with you for ever."* I may grieve Him, as alas, I do almost every day of my life, but I can never grieve Him out of my heart. When He enters, He enters to regenerate and to remain. He is a tenant who can never be evicted, our guest, our Paraclete, until our death or translation when Christ returns. Communion, of course, may be broken, but union can never be severed. And so Augustine was right when he said the Holy Spirit is our perpetual Comforter and our eternal inhabitant.

2. HIS UP-SPRINGING (JOHN 4:14)

Here we have the daily, constant increase of spirituality, as the Holy Spirit is allowed to rise and permeate the entire life of the one regenerated by His power. I do not know whether you have come across this beautiful word in Numbers 21:17, *"Then Israel sang this song, Spring up, O well."* That is holiness: allowing the well to spring up, allowing the Holy Spirit to rise and permeate and dominate every part of the inner life. This is why we sing,

> For still the desert lies
> My thirsty soul before;

Yet living waters rise,
Within me evermore.[3]

3. HIS OUTFLOWING (JOHN 7:37–39)

Out of His body, streams of living water will flow. This great classic passage indicates the further and fuller progress of the Spirit's ministry as He is allowed to have His way in the life of the believer. Entering the life, He strives to fill it with His fullness, and then like Ezekiel's river, He flows on and on and out and out, and everything lives wherever the river flows. Thus the dry wilderness around is refreshed and quickened as the Spirit of God is allowed to flow through the body. So He flows in, He flows through, and then He flows out, making the believer the medium of spiritual blessing and revival.

II. THE SPHERE OF THE THREEFOLD OPERATION OF THE SPIRIT OF GOD

Going a little deeper into our study, we discover that these three phases are related to the three distinct parts of our being. Man is a tripartite being, a trinity in unity. He is made up of spirit, soul, and body. These three are illustrated in the tabernacle of old, where you have the outer court—the body; the holy place—the soul; and the most holy place—the Spirit. All three are brought together for us in one passage of the Holy Bible, namely Genesis 2:7, *"And the Lord God formed man of the dust of the ground, and breathed into his nostrils the breath of life; and man became a living soul."*

1. First of all then, there is the *body*. The Lord God formed the body of Adam out of the dust of the earth. And I believe what is written. Accepting the almightiness of God, I see no

3. John S. B. Monsell, "I Hunger and I Thirst," 1866 (emphasis added).

reason why, in a moment of time, out of a few specks of dust, He could not create the body of Adam. Now the body is the external life. My body connects me with the world without and around. My body is made up of the five senses of hearing, seeing, smelling, tasting, and feeling. The exterior travels to the interior through my body. So because my body connects me with the world without and around, it stands for world-consciousness.

2. Then you have the *soul*. *"Man became a living soul"* (Genesis 2:7). Man has a spirit and a body; he *is* a soul. Man *became* a living soul. Here you have the internal part of the man—the central part. The soul is the hub of man's little universe. It is the holy place. Within the soul, you have all the powers that go to make up personality. In the soul you have three distinct possessions—heart, with which we love; mind, with which we think; and will, with which we decide and act. And so within the soul you have the possessions of imagination, conscience, memory, and reason. The soul is the holy place. My soul is myself. The soul stands for *self-consciousness*.

Now, as you can see, because of its centrality, the soul is acted upon by two sets of attractions. There are the attractions of the world reaching my soul through my body. Then you have the attractions of God reaching the soul through the medium of the spirit.

3. In the next place there is the *spirit*. God *"breathed into his nostrils the breath* [or spirit] *of life"* (Genesis 2:7). Here you have the spiritual part of man, the eternal part. This spirit was the part of God that Adam received in his creation, God's breath. As the body speaks of world-consciousness and the soul of self-consciousness, so the spirit stands for God-consciousness. You speak of the sinner as one who is godless, that is, less or minus God.

What do you mean by that? Why, that there is no connection with God. God is nowhere in all his thoughts. The spirit then stands for God-consciousness. It is the Holy of holies—the part nearest God, and in such you have the faculties for worship and reverence and prayer. When God emphasizes the creation of man, He begins with the body, and that is as it should be. First that which is natural, then that which is spiritual, as the apostle puts it in 1 Corinthians 15:46. But when he comes to the sanctification of the believer in 1 Thessalonians 5:23, he reverses the order, *"I pray God your whole spirit and soul and body be preserved blameless unto the coming of our Lord Jesus Christ."* We are to be sanctified how? Spirit, soul, and body. Man's work of reformation is external. This is why we have schemes for the betterment of man, for the changing of his environment. But as soon as the inner life of a person is changed, the environment is quickly transformed.

James Stalker, in his volume on Christian psychology, tells us that the ancients had a very fitting way of illustrating the threefold part of man. They likened the body to the material framework of a chariot. Then when they came to the soul with all its powers, they likened it to the steeds or the horses harnessed to the chariot. When they thought of the spirit, they looked upon such as the driver, whose keen eye determined the course and whose strong hand held the reins. And you will agree with me when I say that if the spirit part of man is missing or is not functioning, is inoperative, or under the control of evil spirits, as in the case of demonism or spiritism, then you have nothing but chaos and tragedy and death. For God meant the body to be the servant of the soul and the soul the servant of the spirit; and the spirit, soul, and body to be servants of His, and avenues along which the Holy Spirit can travel to a world of need.

Let us now see how these three aspects are related to the three distinct parts of our nature: His incoming into the spirit; His up-springing within the soul; and His outflowing through the body.

1. Let us begin at John 3:6, His *incoming* into our spirit: "*That which is born of the Spirit is spirit.*" What is the implication here? What happened at creation? God made Adam capable of holding fellowship with Himself. But Adam transgressed. And as the result of his transgression, he was expelled from the garden. Communion with God was severed. So you speak of the sinner as one who is spiritually dead. What do you mean by that? Why, the spirit is not functioning. As in material death, there is the separation of the spirit from the body, so in spiritual death there is separation of the spirit from God.

In Genesis 2:17, God said to Adam, "*In the day that thou eatest thereof thou shalt surely die.*" How did Adam die? The day came when he partook of the forbidden fruit, and God said, "*thou shalt surely die.*" Did Adam die physically? No, he lived for many years after. How then did he die? He was expelled from the presence of God. He died spiritually. All through the Old Testament, man is trying to bridge the chasm: "*O that I knew where I might find him*" (Job 23:3). When you come to John 3, you find the chasm bridged. For in regeneration the Holy Spirit resuscitates that dead part and makes it to function. He restores to the believing sinner what he lost by Adam's transgression. That which is born of the Spirit is spirit. And so the work of the Holy Spirit in regeneration is to restore communion, to bring us back into fellowship with God.

It is here that we understand the teaching of the apostle in Romans 8:16, "*The Spirit itself beareth witness with our spirit, that we are the children of God.*" We are brought back again into His presence, and thereby our spirit is made the holiest of all—His seat, His abode, His home. And spirit, indwelt by the Holy Spirit, becomes the fountain head of spirituality and of all spiritual insight. This may be why He has His name the Holy Spirit, seeing His initial work is with the spirit of man. If we could bring this kind of truth before unconverted men and women when we set out to preach the gospel, a foundation would be laid that would make backsliding nearly impossible.

2. In the second place, there is His *up-springing* within our souls. John 4:14 says, "*A well of water springing up.*" The Holy Spirit is not content to remain in my spirit. That is where He begins. Then it is His purpose to rise and permeate the whole life of the believing one. Perhaps we are now ready to understand what the apostle had in mind when he wrote Ephesians 5:18, "*Be filled with the Spirit.*" Sometimes we hear believers in prayer meetings asking God for the Holy Spirit. I think it grieves the Lord when we speak thus. No doubt there is deep need for the unction of the Spirit, but that is something altogether distinct. You can never have any more of a person than that person. You can never accept personality by installments. How do you think I came into this tabernacle; do you think at nine o'clock this morning I sent up my head and then a few moments later my trunk, and a few moments after that my legs and my feet? No, as a person, I entered this tabernacle in my totality. "*If any man have not the Spirit of Christ, he is none of his*" (Romans 8:9). We can never have any more of a person than that person. The Holy Spirit is a person. Therefore, when He entered, He entered in His totality as a person.

But here is the distinction, I have the Holy Spirit, but does He have me? I possess the Spirit; does He possess me? He entered my life; He took up His abode in my spirit. Do I confine Him there? Regenerated! Do I yet live my life according to the precepts of the self-life, or is He rising and filling every part of the soul-life? Is He up-springing within our souls?

You know what happened at Calvary. We read that the veil of the temple was torn in two from the top to the bottom. In the tabernacle of old there were two veils separating three places: there was the veil between the outer court and the holy place, and then there was the veil between the holy place and the most holy place. They were distinct compartments. But at Calvary something happened. The veil was torn in two, which meant that there were no longer veils between but liberty of access into the holiest of all. And the Holy Spirit waits for the rending of the veil between the spirit and the soul, and the soul and the body. Let us not confine Him to our spirit but allow Him to rise and permeate our entire life.

It is here that I understand the teaching of Romans chapters 6 to 8, all of which has to do with the Holy Spirit controlling the self-life of the believer.

3. In the last place there is His *outflowing* through the body, as we see in John 7:37–39: *"Out of his belly shall flow rivers of living water"* (verse 38). The possession of and by the Holy Spirit is not an end but a means to an end. The Holy Spirit does not finish with us. It is the purpose of the Holy Spirit to make the bodies of believers the medium of spiritual quickening, refreshment, and revival. Now let us turn to our Lord's Word at this point. In John 16:7–8 we find Him saying *"I will send him* [the Holy Spirit] *unto you."* This is the implication of the passage: "and when He is come unto you, through you, He will convict the

world of sin and of righteousness and of judgment." This suggests that the work of the Spirit of God in respect to lost souls is largely through human agency. The world cannot understand the truth of the Spirit, Jesus said so in John 14:17, *"Even the Spirit of truth; whom the world cannot receive, because it seeth him not, neither knoweth him: but ye know him; for he dwelleth with you, and shall be in you."*

How is the world to receive the truth of the Spirit? In the same way as they received the truth regarding God the Spirit? The world found it difficult to believe in God, but God came down and indwelt a human body and then the world was able to receive the revelation of God, for Jesus Christ indwelling a human body was the culmination of the revelation of God. He could say, *"He that hath seen me hath seen the Father"* (John 14:9). Now you find Jesus saying of the Holy Spirit *"whom the world cannot receive."* How can it receive Him?

When He fully indwells the human body and works through it, when He is come to you, through you He will convict the world of sin. Link this on to Romans 12:1–2, *"Present your bodies a living sacrifice…"* Why our bodies? Because if we fail to give the Holy Spirit the full control of our bodies, the work in respect to lost souls is frustrated. It is imperative to keep the transmitting line clear. Out from within, out of your body, streams of living water will flow. The tragedy in our churches is this: so many give the Holy Spirit an inlet but not an outlet. The Holy Spirit must have possession, because the Lord Jesus is not here in a body. He has a body, but His body is in glory. He has a real head, real eyes, real lips, real hands, and real feet, but they are all in heaven. And that is why the Holy Spirit must have control of your body and mine. He desires to continue the ministry of Jesus through us.

Oh beloved, this is a truth that will stimulate God's people to greater holy activity for the Savior. Let us tell them that the Holy Spirit is waiting to flow through their eyes, giving them a vision of a perishing world; that He waits to flow through their ears, causing them to listen to the cry of a lost humanity; waiting to flow through their lips in intercession, in confession, and in witnessing; waiting to flow through their hands. Think what the Holy Spirit is able to accomplish through the ten fingers of the two hands. I know my limitations; I am more than ever conscious of them; but I long to have fingers fully controlled by the Holy Spirit, that through them, by means of the printed page, I might express truth divine.

You think of the consecrated fingers—fingers through which the Holy Spirit was flowing. A shut-in can be visited, and a bunch of flowers can be carried with the hand, or a gospel message, and that soul may be wonderfully blessed and enriched. And if people have gold, through the surrender of their consecrated money, the Holy Spirit can flow to others in their need. And He can flow through our feet. There may be some here today, in whom the Holy Spirit is going to travel to the ends of the earth with the message of Jesus and His love. Let us never forget that our body is the temple of the Holy Spirit and through it He strives to reveal the glory of God.

RECEPTACLE CHRISTIANS

This brings me to my concluding thought. There are two kinds of Christians. You have in the first place what I call the receptacle Christian. A jug is receptacle. It retains what it receives.

A receptacle Christian is always a hindrance, no matter where you find him. The Dead Sea received its name because it was forever receiving the life-giving water from the surrounding hills and mountains and retaining all that it received. God save us from functioning as "Dead Sea" Christians. If water is not flowing, it becomes stagnant. Some people are determined to attend every convention, and we often see the same old faces. They sit and listen and drink in the truth. They receive it and receive it—the wonder is, they never burst. I trust you will not be a receptacle Christian, but what you receive you will seek to transmit to others.

CHANNEL CHRISTIANS

Then you have the channel Christians. Now, a channel is open at both ends. Suppose I had a piece of pipe here. There is no need for that pipe to be fashioned of gold. No matter how common and ordinary the material, so long as it is clean and useable. I could fix one end of that pipe to a vast reservoir of life-giving water and then through it I would supply the thirsty souls in the community. The pipe cannot hold very much. It can overflow a great deal. What flows in, flows through, and then flows out, Are we channel Christians?

> Channels only, blessed Master,
> But with all Thy wondrous power
> Flowing through us, Thou canst use us,
> Every day and every hour."[4]

God help us to be open at both ends—open at the Godward end, forever receiving what the Lord may have for us; open at the world end, transmitting what we receive. You have a piece of the world to influence, and if your body is not fully surrendered

4. Mary E. Maxwell, "Channels Only," 1900.

to the Holy Spirit, then His work is frustrated in that piece of the world that you represent. Out of your body streams of living water will flow.

Saintly Bishop Moule went to Rome for a holiday. While there, he was intrigued by a company of workmen who were excavating a ruin. He stopped alongside one of the workmen who was having difficulty with a huge boulder. It was covered with the dust and dirt of centuries. But he labored away steadily with that pick, and as he removed the boulder, immediately there issued forth a life-giving spring. It had been there all the time, but buried and confined. The moment the boulder with its dirt and rubbish was removed, the spring expressed itself. And you know as well as I do that there are many who have the well within. We could never doubt the fact of their regeneration, but the boulder prevents the well of living water from flowing out and expressing Him. The boulder is there, covered over with the dirt and rubbish of carnality and worldliness and selfishness. It may be that we are conscious of the boulder. We are born again by the Spirit, but He is not having expression. God help us to let the boulder go so that out of us rivers of living water may flow.

CHAPTER THREE:

THE HOLY SPIRIT IN THE LIFE OF THE LORD JESUS

The New Testament reveals a holy intimacy existing between the Lord Jesus and the divine Spirit. These two are one. The phrase that we have in Matthew 12:28, *"I…by the Spirit,"* characterizes not only the casting out of demons but our Lord's every action; for His entire life was imbued with the Holy Spirit. There are two introductory thoughts, however, to bear in mind before we come to our theme proper:

First, in His incarnation, our Lord emptied Himself in that He became subject to the Father's will and dependent upon the Holy Spirit. As you think of His humanity, you cannot get away from these two thoughts. Everything was referred to the Father. He lived in that wonderful realm of His Father's will, and all things were regulated by such. In His humiliation

He was likewise dependent upon the Spirit. *"I...by the Spirit of God."* And in these two traits He has left us an example that we should follow His steps. We can never be fruitful in service unless we learn how to be subject to the Father and be dependent upon the Spirit.

The second thought is, when our Lord was here during the days of His flesh, the Holy Spirit seemed to exclusively occupy the Lord Jesus. After His wondrous birth by the Holy Spirit, you never have any reference to the Holy Spirit having anything to do with any other individual, until after our Lord's resurrection when, breathing upon His disciples, He said, *"Receive ye the Holy Ghost"* (John 20:22). I wonder if this thought has ever struck you while reading the gospel story. After our Lord's incarnation, you have no reference in the Gospels to the Holy Spirit having anything to do with any other individual. He concentrated on our blessed Lord. With this fact in mind, the message of the Savior in John 7:39 is made very clear, the Holy Spirit was not yet given unto men: *"But this spake he of the Spirit, which they that believe on him should receive: for the Holy Ghost was not yet given; because that Jesus was not yet glorified."* There had to be one man who could receive the Holy Spirit in His fullness before that gracious Holy Spirit could be poured out upon men and women in the plentitude of power. And here, for the first time, in the Lord Jesus, is Man able to receive the Holy Spirit of God in His entirety.

Coming to our theme, then, we are impressed with the beautiful blending, merging, infusing, or incorporating—as we read the New Testament—of the Holy Spirit and the Lord Jesus. They seem to be one. It is perfectly true that the Holy Spirit is Jesus' other self. He could say, in the days of His flesh, *"I and the Father are one"* (John 10:30 RSV). It is also true that the Holy Spirit and He are one. The fine flour, unleavened, was mingled with oil. Let me suggest to you how you can make this study very practical in your own private meditation.

I. OUR LORD WAS PROPHESIED BY THE HOLY SPIRIT

Take 1 Peter 1:11, where we read, "*Searching what, or what manner of time the Spirit of Christ which was in them did signify, when it testified beforehand the sufferings of Christ, and the glory that should follow,*" and link this onto 2 Peter 1:20–21, where the apostle tells us that "*Knowing this first, that no prophecy of the scripture is of any private interpretation. For the prophecy came not in old time by the will of man: but holy men of God spake as they were moved by the Holy Spirit.*"

Surely these passages teach that in the New Testament the Holy Spirit was preparing the way for the Lord Jesus. It was because the prophets wrote under the inspiration of the divine Spirit that they gave witness to the Lord Jesus. So in the days of His flesh, our Lord could lay hold of the Old Testament and expound from it the things concerning Himself. "*Lo, I come (in the volume of the book it is written of me)*" (Hebrews 10:7). The great burden of the Holy Spirit in the making of the Old Testament was to prepare the way for the Lord.

We speak about John the Baptist being the forerunner of Jesus, and so he was; but in the ancient Scriptures the Holy Spirit, like a heavenly forerunner of Christ, points to the Lamb of God.

In the Old Testament we have wonderful portraits of the Lord Jesus. In Genesis 3:15 there is the first promise of redemption, the seed of the woman nullifying the seed of the serpent:

"And I will put enmity between thee and the woman, and between thy seed and her seed; it shall bruise thy head, and thou shalt bruise his heel." And in all the types, rituals, and experiences associated with God's ancient people, the Lord Jesus is revealed.

Then, as the time drew near for our Lord to step aside from the ivory palaces into this world of woe, the Holy Spirit was especially active in the minds of devout men. For example, there is Zacharias' divine prophecy regarding Christ. Then there was Simeon, that devout saint, who had it revealed unto him by the Holy Spirit that he should not die until he had seen the Lord's Christ. Thus from the time of the first promise of redemption up to the time of our Lord's birth, the Holy Spirit was preparing the way for Him.

And as the Spirit prepared the way for the first advent, so in these last days He is moving among the people of God, preparing them for our Lord's second coming.

II. OUR LORD WAS BORN OF THE HOLY SPIRIT

In the next place we discover from Holy Bible that Jesus was born of the Holy Spirit. Matthew 1:18 says, *"Now the birth of Jesus Christ was on this wise: When as His mother Mary was espoused to Joseph, before they came together, she was found with child of the Holy Ghost."* Here we find ourselves in the presence of mystery, for although we cannot explain the birth of our blessed Lord, we do believe the fact that He had a human mother, but that He did not have a human father. He was conceived of the Holy Spirit and born of the Virgin Mary. Job has this question, *"How can he be clean that is born of a woman?"* (Job 25:4). Well, Jesus was born of a woman and yet He was clean. Mary was a sinner and recognized her need of a Savior: *"My spirit hath rejoiced in God my Saviour*" (Luke 1:47). But although a sinner, she gave birth to One who was sinless. Although Jesus was born of a woman, yet nevertheless He was clean; and if we do not accept the virgin birth of our Lord, then we never can explain His presence among men as a sinless Being.

How this could be, we cannot explain, for great is the mystery of godliness, but think of this as you meditate upon the virgin birth of Christ: in the incarnation, the Holy Spirit added to our Lord's already existing divine nature, a human nature. But in our new birth, the reverse takes place; for the Holy Spirit, in the hour of regeneration, adds to our existing human nature the divine nature, making us thereby partakers of the divine nature. John reminds us that as "*he is, so are we in this world*" (1 John 4:17), and we cannot think of the incarnation without being reminded of our own new birth, for "*of His own will begat he us*" (James 1:18). We are born not of the will of the flesh, but of God, born of the Word of Truth and by the Spirit of God. In the epistle to the Galatians, Paul relates his natural and spiritual birth and writes thus, "*It pleased God...to reveal his Son in me*" (Galatians 1:15–16). Further, he reminds the Galatians that he labors for them in travail until Christ be formed in them. As we ponder the mystery of life and of the life eternal, may we make the words we so often sing the prayer of our hearts: "O Jesus Christ grow Thou in me."[5]

III. OUR LORD WAS JUSTIFIED BY THE HOLY SPIRIT

In the next place, we discover Jesus was justified by the Spirit. 1 Timothy 3:16 says, "*God was manifest in the flesh, justified in the Spirit, seen of angels,*" etc. "*Manifest in the flesh,*" that refers to His incarnation. But where can we place this phrase,

5. J. C. Lavater, "O Jesus Christ, Grow Thou in Me," 1780.

"*justified in the Spirit*"? It seems to me that we can lay hold of that phrase and stretch it right over those thirty silent years lived out in His humble home in Nazareth. After His birth, we have only one glimpse of Christ until He reaches the age of thirty, namely, at the age of twelve, when we find Him in the temple asking and answering questions. Well, what happened right through that long period? Jesus was justified by the Spirit. He lived in a home in which He was not understood; at the early age of twelve, He had to rebuke His mother, saying, "*Wist ye not that I must be about my Father's business?*" (Luke 2:49).

After the legal marriage of Joseph and Mary, children came into the home along the avenue of natural generation, and as they grew up with the Lord, they did not understand why He was in the world and what His mission was. Thus His brothers did not believe in Him. He moved among them as a kind of mystery. Yet all through those thirty years, He was justified by the Spirit. He had not the justification of others, but He did enjoy the justification of the Holy Spirit. The Holy Spirit said, "Amen" to all that Jesus said and accomplished.

Although people may misunderstand us and misconstrue our motives, if we have the justification or vindication of the Spirit, then we can afford to be silent. There is no reason to concern ourselves about what people say or think. Our reputation is what people think of us; character is what God thinks of us. Jesus "*made himself of no reputation*" (Philippians 2:7). He was very careful, however, about His character, saying, "*The Father hath not left me alone; for I do always those things that please him*" (John 8:29). And if, like Christ, we are careful regarding our character, then we can afford to be independent regarding our reputation.

IV. OUR LORD WAS ANOINTED WITH THE HOLY SPIRIT

Further, we read that Jesus was anointed with the Holy Spirit. *"And Jesus, when he was baptized, went up straightway out of the water: and lo, the heavens were opened unto Him, and he saw the Spirit of God descending like a dove, and lighting upon him"* (Matthew 3:16). The Lord laid hold of an Old Testament prophecy and related it to Himself, *"I have put my spirit upon him"* (Isaiah 42:1). Here He stands at the age of thirty with John at Jordan, and as He faces His short ministry of three and a half years, He receives this distinctive anointing with the Spirit. Remember that He was born of the Spirit; He enjoyed the vindication of the Spirit through those silent years lived out in Nazareth. But now, before He takes up His ministry, He requires this distinctive anointing of the Spirit.

Have we come to that place in our spiritual experience? We can never be fruitful unless we stand with Jesus at Jordan and receive the anointing of the Holy Spirit for service. He can be in you and yet not upon you. He was within our Lord for He was born of the Spirit and justified by the Spirit, but now at Jordan He comes upon Christ and endues Him for the ministry awaiting Him.

V. OUR LORD WAS LED OF THE HOLY SPIRIT

The next phase of this wondrous union is found in Matthew 4:1, *"Then was Jesus led up of the Spirit into the wilderness to be tempted of the devil."* Now, it may be that we are perplexed by this phase of the mystical association of the Spirit with Christ. After the anointing at Jordan, we would have expected Jesus to go out in the power of the Spirit and perform miracles, making it evident thereby that He had received this wonderful endowment. But no, after the anointing He goes into the wilderness to be tempted. Let me say this to you: if God meets with you and brings you into some deep spiritual experience, look out for the enemy of your soul, for he ever comes on the back of some exalted spiritual experience. From Jordan, Jesus went into the wilderness to be tempted of the devil.

Often God meets with souls at some holy convocation, and their eyes are opened. Their spiritual life is deepened, and they have a vision of a life of full, complete surrender to the Lord. Out they go, feeling as if they were in the seventh heaven. With hearts filled with unspeakable joy, they seem to walk on air. Then the next day or so, the enemy seems to come to them with renewed force, and they experience a time of terrific temptation. Doubt emerges regarding the validity of the spiritual experience they had when the Lord drew near. But this experience of Christ should safeguard us; Jesus was led into the wilderness to be tempted of the devil. He must know the full weight and strength of the foe if He would deliver those tempted by the enemy.

Twice over, you have that word *"led"* in our Lord's ministry: here in the beginning, *"led up of the Spirit,"* and in the end of His ministry, *"they led him out to crucify him"* (Mark 15:20). There is always a cross for the Spirit-filled, Spirit-led believer.

VI. OUR LORD WAS EMPOWERED BY THE HOLY SPIRIT

We have now reached a blessed phase of this mysterious union. In the next place, Jesus was empowered by the Spirit:

> *And Jesus returned in the power of the Spirit into Galilee: and there went out a fame of him through all the region round about. And he taught in their synagogues, being glorified of all. And he came to Nazareth, where he had been brought up: and, as his custom was, he went into the synagogue on the sabbath day, and stood up for to read. And there was delivered unto him the book of the prophet Esaias. And when he had opened the book, he found the place where it was written, The Spirit of the Lord is upon me, because he hath anointed me to preach the gospel to the poor; he hath sent me to heal the brokenhearted, to preach deliverance to the captives, and recovering of sight to the blind, to set at liberty them that are bruised.*
>
> (Luke 4:14–18)

Mark the association: first Jordan with its anointing, then the wilderness with its testing. And after the victory of the wilderness, there came the manifestation of divine power. At Jordan, the Holy Spirit came upon Jesus in the form of a dove, but after the dove, there came the devil; and after the devil, there was the dynamic, for Jesus returned into Galilee in the power of the Spirit. Now He could meet the foe, for He conquered him in the wilderness in that grim battle, proving Himself, thereby, the glorious Victor. The Spirit energized Christ and gave Him power over sin, Satan, and sickness. By the Spirit of God, He exercised His miraculous ministry.

VII. OUR LORD WAS GLADDENED BY THE HOLY SPIRIT

Further, we read that Jesus was gladdened by the Holy Spirit. I wonder if you ever thought of that passage in Luke

10:21, *"In that hour Jesus rejoiced in spirit."* The word *spirit* has a small *s* as if to infer that it was in His own spirit that He rejoiced, but the Revised Version says, *"He* [Jesus] *rejoiced in the Holy Spirit"* (RV). Weymouth translates it, *"Jesus Christ was filled by the Holy Spirit with rapturous joy."* It is quite true that Jesus was the Man of Sorrows and the One acquainted with grief, but with it let us not forget, He was *"anointed...with the oil of gladness above* [His] *fellows"* (Hebrews 1:9). Thus the Holy Spirit was the source of our Lord's joy. He was filled with rapturous joy by the Holy Spirit.

The Holy Spirit and joy are united in the New Testament. Paul tells us that we are to *"joy in the Holy Ghost"* (Romans 14:17). On the day of Pentecost when the Spirit of God fell upon those waiting disciples, they became God-intoxicated men, so much so that those around them said, *"These men are full of new wine"* (Acts 2:13). There was a wonderful joy about them that they did not possess before. Then when they came to suffer for the Lord in the early part of Acts, we read that they were *"filled with joy, and with the Holy Ghost"* (Acts 13:52).

We need to know more of the Holy Spirit as the source of joy. There is a great difference between joy and happiness. Happiness, as the word suggests, depends upon what happens. If certain things do not happen, then we are not very happy. Joy, however, is independent of all circumstances. This is why Paul and Silas, in prison with backs so sore and bleeding, could sing praises unto God. They knew what it was to have the joy of the Holy Spirit possessing them. They were victorious over their circumstances. If we had been there, perhaps we would not have had grace to sing praises to God. These men, dominated and possessed by the Holy Spirit, were filled with joy. Let us learn how to joy in God through our Lord Jesus Christ.

VIII. OUR LORD DIED BY THE SPIRIT

In the next place we read that Jesus died by the Spirit. This brings us to that wonderful verse in Hebrews 9:14, *"Christ, who through the eternal Spirit, offered himself without spot to God."* See how wonderfully the Holy Spirit upheld and sustained the Lord Jesus from the very time of His birth. He was responsible for our Lord's sinless body, and then He filled that body, making possible our Lord's miraculous ministry. Now as He goes to die, the same Spirit is there enabling Him to suffer in our place.

"Through the eternal Spirit." I wonder if we realize this as we ought: that in the Holy Spirit, we have in the world today the only living witness of the sufferings of Christ. He was there when Jesus died. When Peter, in Acts 5:32, speaks about the crucifixion, he refers to men who slew Jesus and hanged Him on the tree, and goes on to say, *"and we are His witnesses of these things* [namely, the sufferings of Christ]; *and so is also the Holy Ghost, whom God hath given to them that obey him."* The first generation of witnesses passed away nearly nineteen hundred years ago, but in the Holy Spirit we have the only remaining witness to the death of Christ. He was there as our Lord expired; it was the Holy Spirit who enabled Jesus to die as our substitute. This greatly encourages me as a preacher, for when I stand before an unconverted audience and preach the cross, if I depend upon the Holy Spirit, He will bless and use such preaching for the conversion of my hearers.

If I am true to the redemption message, the Holy Spirit will visualize the sufferings of Christ, thereby making the preaching of the cross the means of salvation. Jesus died by the Spirit, and in a spiritual way we can only die in the same fashion. We are exhorted by Paul to *"mortify therefore your members which are upon the earth; fornication, uncleanness, inordinate affection, evil concupiscence, and covetousness, which is idolatry"* (Colossians 3:5). How can we put to death the deeds of the body? *"By the Spirit"* (Galatians 5:16).

IX. OUR LORD WAS RAISED BY THE HOLY SPIRIT

Further, Jesus was raised by the Spirit. *"But if the Spirit of him that raised up Jesus from the dead dwell in you, he that raised up Christ from the dead shall also quicken your mortal bodies by his Spirit that dwelleth in you"* (Romans 8:11). This corresponds with 1 Peter 3:18, which says, *"For Christ also hath once suffered for sins, the just for the unjust, that he might bring us to God, being put to death in the flesh, but quickened by the Spirit."* So the Holy Spirit did not leave Jesus after He uttered His last cry and commended His Spirit to God. True, He was responsible for our Lord's body and did possess and uphold the Savior as He died. Tender hands then took the dead body of Jesus from the cross and placed it in the tomb. Where do you think the Holy Spirit was when Jesus was in the tomb? I have a feeling that the Holy Spirit was guarding the precious body of Jesus, for it was He who made possible its resurrection.

The Roman government had a seal on the outside of the tomb, but God had His seal within the tomb, for the Holy Spirit is the seal—*"sealed* [with the Holy Spirit] *unto the day of redemption"* (Ephesians 4:30). He was there. Thus, on the third day, with the rolling away of the stone, the Holy Spirit quickened the body of Jesus and He was raised. As the Spirit of life, He was responsible for our Lord's resurrection.

And it is He who quickens us, spiritually, physically, mentally. He is the pledge of our physical resurrection, for we are *"sealed* [with the Holy Spirit] *until the day of redemption,"* which means the redemption of the body. I have a redeemed spirit, but that redeemed spirit is a prisoner of hope. It is in the old body. What I need is a new body corresponding with the new life within. The Holy Spirit, then, is the pledge of the redemption of the body. Because the Spirit indwells me, I know that I am to be raised and have a body that corresponds with the redeemed spirit within.

X. OUR LORD GAVE COMMANDMENTS BY THE HOLY SPIRIT

The last phase of this wondrous union is in Acts 1:2, *"Until the day in which he was taken up, after that he through the Holy Ghost had given commandments unto the apostles whom he had chosen."* Before He left His own, He committed unto them the Word they were to proclaim, and receiving that inspired message from the lips of Jesus, they went forth. After Pentecost they built upon the Word, and all through the church age, the same Spirit-inspired message has ever been proclaimed.

Suffer a practical word in conclusion. John tells us in 1 John 2:6, *"He that saith he abideth in him ought himself also so to walk, even as He walked."* How did Jesus walk? He walked in the Spirit. And so, as you have this holy intimacy between Christ and the Spirit, in like manner we must allow all our thoughts, our words, our feelings, our actions, and our pursuits to be saturated, permeated through and through, with the Holy Spirit. Oh, to be as full of the Spirit as Jesus was! Let us believe and claim the promise, *"But ye shall receive power, after that the Holy Ghost is come upon you"* (Acts 1:8). Recognize, as you read this promise, that the power is in the Person. The power is the Person. God never gives us power apart from the Person. Sometimes Christians pray and plead for power as though God has some mysterious energy to bestow. The Holy Spirit Himself is the power; the Holy Spirit coming upon you. Believe and claim the promise.

Then forsake all known sin. Because He is the Spirit of holiness, everything alien to His will must be forsaken. There must be nothing contrary to His holy mind and will within the life. Finally we must learn how to respond immediately to the least whisper of His voice.

Whatsoever is not of faith is sin. Look upon doubt, in regard to a thing being right, as the voice of the Spirit. If there is any particular habit in your life you have a doubt about, then treat doubt as the mind of the Spirit.

Give the Holy Spirit the benefit of the doubt! "*Whatsoever He saith unto you, do it*" (John 2:5). Thus as you cultivate the habit of obeying the Spirit of God, you will come to know more of this mysterious union between Christ and the Spirit, and between the Holy Spirit and those who love and know the Redeemer.

CHAPTER FOUR:

THE HOLY SPIRIT AND SERVICE

Spiritual Atmospherics" would be a more fitting title for this study, seeing that we have reached a consideration of what we call the "atmosphere" of a meeting. Atmosphere is an invisible factor to be reckoned with in all true service for God. Deficient understanding of this cripples our usefulness. The presence of Satan and of satanic influences in centers of worship and ministry is a fact we are apt to forget. And, as the best of assemblies cannot exclude the devil who, from old, has had the power to present himself with the sons of God as they come into the presence of God, it behooves us not to be ignorant of his devices.

I. THE FORCES WITHIN ATMOSPHERE

Christians, generally speaking, do not sufficiently realize the importance of "atmosphere." They seem to forget that every meeting is a veritable battlefield with spiritual powers in deadly combat. So often people congregate for a mere service all unconscious of the vital issues at stake. There is prevailing ignorance regarding the competent parts of this mystic element we term "atmosphere." There are, at least, three forces operating, and we only get the very best out of our work as we understand their exact nature.

HEAVENLY FORCES

The whole weight of the blessed Trinity is concentrated upon the glory of God in and through the salvation and sanctification of souls. Along with such, there is the service of the unfallen angelic host. It is not sentimental to believe in the ministry of angels. If there is joy over sinners repenting, surely they must be present to witness such repentance.

HELLISH FORCES

Then we have satanic influences at work in every gathering of people. Satan is more alive to the importance of atmosphere than we give him credit for. Every time, he is out to wreck the power of true spiritual work. One has said that when Satan goes to church he goes to *prey* (not pray). May we never aid him! As men and women meet in the name of the Lord, the devil marshals all his satanic forces together, that he might destroy the work of the Trinity on behalf of souls as the Word is preached. This is made very clear to us in the descriptions given to us of Satan. Think of who he is! Take up your concordance and look over his titles. He is the prince of demons. He is referred to as the enemy sowing tares among the wheat, so when you stand up and try to give the people wheat, the enemy is there seeking to scatter tares amidst the wheat. He is the prince of the power of the air and also the prince of this world and the leader of vast spiritual fallen hosts. Thus heavenly and hellish powers are in deadly combat.

HUMAN FORCES

In the next place, there are human forces at work, and this brings us to the part we play as we meet together. Coming to ourselves, we discover a variety of human elements helping to form what we call atmosphere. We cannot explain it, but we all know what we mean by it. We go into a service, and if tense with the power of God, we leave, saying, "What a wonderful atmosphere!" Or we go into one that is cold and dead, and we come away remarking, "There was no atmosphere there at all." No blessing is derived, simply because of the absence of a right atmosphere.

When we come together it is essential for us to realize that we ourselves are the deciding factor as to which force is going to control, heavenly or hellish. Suppose people could be instructed along these lines and informed that when they come together they contribute the deciding factor as to which force is going to control, heavenly or hellish, what a change in service would be experienced. This is a very solemn thought. To think that I, more or less, hold the balance between heaven and hell—that I can either help the Lord or assist the enemy as he strives to wreck the atmosphere. We hold the balance between the two. We either help the Lord or the devil. We either assist the Savior or the serpent. We are either on the side of the angels or on the side of the demons. I think it would revolutionize Christian work if we could tell Christian people as they meet in the Lord's name, that they hold the balance between heavenly forces and hellish forces. Why? It is because so many professing Christians are not in touch with the Lord, and have, in some way or another, yielded to Satan, that when they come together in the meeting there is so little result.

II. THE VALUE OF ATMOSPHERE

Let us now consider the value of the atmosphere to those who preach, to those who hear, and to the Holy Spirit. First, think of the value of the right atmosphere to those who preach. A true witness is ever susceptible regarding the atmosphere of a meeting. If you are in touch with the Lord, you can sense the atmosphere of a meeting after you have been in it for two or three minutes. Many powerful messages have been blasted through the absence of the right atmosphere believers failed to produce. I believe that with all my heart. Many a minister of the gospel has been chilled by the wintry, depressing air blowing around him in the house of God, as he has sought to give the divine message.

Now, if we are to have liberty in the declaration of the message, we must have the atmosphere in which to hold forth the word the Holy Spirit has impressed upon our minds, and when this atmosphere is present, we have a sense of our own unworthiness, and yet the realization that we are in the presence of God and are speaking with divine authority.

Secondly, think of the importance to those who hear. Spiritual freedom in preaching is evidence of receptivity in the hearer. When you have liberty, you know that everything is working together for good in that meeting, and that because of a right atmosphere everything is being drawn out of you. If there is no freedom in the meeting, you are bound in spirit and sometimes leave the meeting threatening never to preach again.

If unsaved men and women in a meeting are to be convicted of their need, and if they are to be brought to a realization of the saving grace of the Lord, there must be the atmosphere in which the Holy Spirit will make that conviction possible. Atmosphere is of great value to those who hear.

In the last place, atmosphere is of great value to the Holy Spirit. The Holy Spirit is the direct Agent between our heart and the Lord, let us remember. The church has lost the truth regarding the lordship of the Spirit. He is the administrator of the affairs of the church. When you go to the book of Acts, you find the early church so full of vitality that every time they came together, something happened. Why? Because they recognized the lordship of the Spirit. They gave the Holy Spirit the atmosphere in which He could work. This is why we read that when Peter preached the Word, the Holy Spirit fell upon the company and they were pricked to the heart. And wherever the lordship of the Spirit is recognized, meetings are tense with His power and Christian work becomes fatal to the devil. The value of a right atmosphere, then, is seen in that preacher, hearer, and the Holy Spirit, all profit when there is recognition of these important principles.

III. HINDRANCE TO A RIGHT ATMOSPHERE

The hindrances to a right atmosphere operate in many ways. The worker may be out of touch. The message may be out of touch. The plan may be out of touch. The hearer may be out of touch. Let us look at each of these.

1. *The worker may be out of touch.* By the term "worker," I include the preacher, teacher, or singer, and all those who take any public part in the conducting of a meeting. We must realize

it is vastly important to have the life behind the message. Our own spiritual experience is of paramount importance. A minister's life is the life of his ministry. This is true in respect of any Christian worker. The worker's life is the life of his work. You may be able to stand before others and give a well-ordered and even spiritual message and yet never know deep heart sanctity. It is sadly possible to preach truth beyond our own experience. If I depend upon my gifts, upon any eloquence I may have, upon any talent or ability the Lord has bestowed upon me, thinking that my service is going to tell for God, when privately I am careless, prayer-less, and defeated, I make a fatal mistake. What the Holy Spirit lays hold of and uses in a meeting is not so much the Word but the life pulsating behind it. It is here that we can understand John 1:4, "*The life was the light of men,*" and the light always illuminates. The life behind the message never fails to achieve the divine purpose.

2. In the second place, *the message may be out of touch.* We must strive not to give our best but God's best, and God's best is found in His Word. The Holy Spirit has not promised to bless popular themes, discussions of politics and economics, or sermons on current topics. He always rides in triumph in His own chariot. So often we have seen a meeting wrecked because a man came to that meeting with a message not in keeping with the mind of God. The message was out of touch.

Of course, you know you ought to repeat your old sermons. If God burns a message into your heart, you must repeat it. D.L. Moody said he always preached a sermon better after the twentieth time. But here is the tragedy—so many men repeat old sermons without seeking a re-baptism of divine power. If we say, as we go over old sermons, "Oh well, I'll take this; I've spoken on that before," and give out an old message without seeking a fresh baptism of divine power, the sermon will fall dead and flat upon our hearers. The Holy Spirit has no opportunity. The message is out of touch.

3. Third, *the plan may be out of touch.* So often there is carelessness about the plan of meeting. I was in a conference not long ago where the leader rushed in from the outside, was busy here and there, and stood, just before the meeting, fumbling through a book, trying to find suitable hymns. That is not the way to create atmosphere in which the Holy Spirit is able to work. And if we depend upon self-created methods merely, we work with tools the Holy Spirit is not able to use.

Sometimes I think it would be a marvelous thing if the Holy Spirit would break up all our plans and take full control. Often He is organized out of work bearing the name of "Christian."

4. *The hearer may be out of touch.* I want you to emphasize this when you find yourself in your own sphere, preaching and teaching. There are some people who are a valuable asset in every meeting they attend, because they concentrate upon the issues at stake, and they pray the preacher through to victory. Often in my ministry, I used to look from the pulpit, and when I saw certain people in the pew I felt relieved. I knew they would be praying for me, striving to keep back the evil forces. When they were missing, I had a kind of lost feeling inside. Their influence was missing if they were not sitting in their accustomed place. Some believers, then, are a valuable asset. Others are a hindrance to the Holy Spirit, and it would be better for all concerned if they stayed away, simply because of their coldness, carnality, or unspiritual frame of mind. They come together so unconscious of the vital issues at stake. They bring into the atmosphere that which militates against the blessing of God and the work of the Trinity on behalf of souls.

IV. THE SECURING OF ATMOSPHERE

Concerning the securing of a right atmosphere, there are three things to remember: right attitude before the service, right attitude while present in the service, and right attitude after the service. Just a word or two concerning these:

1. There must be a right attitude when we come together. There is a vital connection between our home life and our personal service. We know that.

Suppose I leave home in a wrong spirit. I was somewhat critical, snappy, ruffled, and prayer-less. What can I expect when I come into my meeting? I may have ability to preach a good sermon, but the Holy Spirit has not very much to work upon, seeing that I did not bring with me that which contributes to the mystic element known as atmosphere.

So often when people are on the way to church, they are guilty of inattention; they engage in frivolous conversation and gossip, thus, when they arrive at a given place of worship or ministry, they have brought an evil brood of demons with them. It is important to emphasize that. We must have a right attitude before we come to a meeting. Some of you are ministers. Impress upon your people that if they jump out of bed hurriedly and rush all the way to church, they will only get out of the church service what they put into it. Remind them that they are not going to put anything into it in that careless, prayer-less fashion.

2. Further, I am confident of this, that our gatherings would be more profitable and fruitful if we were more careful about maintaining a spiritual atmosphere while present. Sometimes in the few minutes before a service starts, there is a tremendous clatter of tongues. The beginning of the service suggests the rabble of the market rather than the house of God, where we

are about to meet with the Lord Most High. So often, in the first few moments of a service, people are anxious to see who is there. Their eyes are all over the church, seeing how many are present or who is absent, and what kind of new clothes people are wearing. There must be a right attitude while present, if the Spirit is to be unhindered.

How do you suppose a right atmosphere, a spiritual atmosphere, is created? Not by gifted singing, not by gifted playing, not by the ministry of the song leader, and not entirely by eloquent preaching. A spiritual atmosphere is created by a company of spiritually minded people bent on dispossessing Satan. I repeat: A spiritual atmosphere is created by a company of spiritually minded people bent on dispossessing Satan.

Often we are wrong in our approach. I think of a large evangelistic effort by a song leader who would spend the first forty-five minutes of every meeting singing choruses, choruses, choruses. All sorts of tricks were resorted to in order to work up the meeting. I asked the song leader, "Why do you do that?" He replied, "Oh, we are trying to sing these choruses in several ways to create an atmosphere." But this is not the method the Spirit blesses. The only way by which we can create a spiritual atmosphere is in the way I have indicated, namely, by spiritually minded people bent on dispossessing Satan and giving God, thereby, an opportunity to display His power. It is our responsibility to urge people to be very prayerful and reverent while they tarry together in the house of God.

3. In the next place, there must be a right attitude after the meeting. As much depends for spiritual success upon our attitude after the meeting as before it, or during the service. I wonder if we really believe this. Sometimes I have left a meeting absolutely distressed. One has tried to put their soul into the

message and come to the help of the Lord against the mighty, only to find the believers leaving the meeting acting as if they were never in the Lord's presence at all. In this way the enemy is helped to sow tares among the wheat. His business is to blast the influence of all good seed. The fowls of the air are at the door, hovering around to pluck up the seed and destroy it.

I speak to my own heart when I say that often the preacher loses his influence after delivering a powerful message by his frivolous talk and careless attitude. I have known preachers to stand on the platform and bring men and women so near God that His very presence was realized, and then, five minutes after the meeting, murder the influence that was created.

I am sure you will agree with me when I remark that when we have had a great time in the service of the Lord, have felt Him working, and were conscious of His nearness, that we felt like running away and hiding ourselves, lest we should destroy our own influence by any injudicious talking or acting.

Let me indicate in closing one or two ways to combat Satan's supremacy and overthrow it. It is blessed to know that we can defeat Satan and help thereby to produce a spiritual atmosphere in every meeting we attend. We either help or hinder the Lord.

As we enter the portal of a church or place of meeting, we must say to ourselves, "Who is going to dominate this meeting? On whose side am I? Am I going to help the Lord or the devil? The Lord is present. Satan is present. I hold the balance between the two. May I have the grace to come to the help of the Lord against the mighty."

Let us see how we can defeat Satan. First, we must never yield to any satanic influence. We must say to ourselves, "I will refuse to yield to his distractions." We can guard ourselves in this direction in several ways. For example, we must see to it that we are not willing party to Satan's company. We cannot hinder his coming with us. When the angels came to present themselves before the Lord, Satan came also among them. They were not a willing party to his coming, however. We must come to our work in a holy frame of mind. If we resist the devil he will flee from us. That is God's Word. It is not too good to be true. If we resist the devil, he cringes before us as a defeated foe.

At the meeting, realizing he is present, we must not overrate his power. We are sometimes guilty of overrating the devil's power. Often people underrate his power. Remember that Satan is present in some form or another, there to capture man's soul, but that he is only like a dog on a leash, and that, if we are in vital touch with the Lord, we can resist the power of Satan.

Consider in this connection to Job 2:1, *"And Satan came also among them to present himself before the Lord."* A good Bible has in the margin this phrase: "And Satan was in the midst"—in the midst of the angels. I take this phrase in the margin and link it to a familiar phrase in the Gospels, *"Where two or three are gathered together in my name, there am I in the midst of them"* (Matthew 18:20). Satan is in the midst. Yes, but the Lord is also in the midst, and He is well able to overcome the enemy of souls if we give Him every opportunity.

Then, of course, we must refuse to yield to any satanic influence while present. You are sitting in a meeting, perhaps, and the devil makes you critical regarding the preacher; or while you are sitting there you see somebody with whom you are not altogether on good terms, and the devil fills your mind with all kinds of thoughts regarding that person. That is distraction, and the devil is a master in creating distraction. It has been his business for over six thousand years, and he has the accumulated wisdom of the centuries and knows how to fill our minds with roving thoughts, keeping us from the main issue in any given meeting.

May we never forget that if the human is in league with the heavenly, he or she can defeat the hellish every time. We have the prerogative, as well as the Savior, of saying to the devil, "*Get thee behind me, Satan*" (Matthew 16:23). And if we exercise our prerogative, then the devil can never make us sin against our will.

Then urge people as they gather together to claim victory on the ground of the cross. I am very fond of Revelation 12:10–11:

> *And I heard a loud voice saying in heaven, Now is come salvation, and strength, and the kingdom of our God, and the power of his Christ: for the accuser of our brethren is cast down, which accused them before our God day and night. And they overcame him by the blood of the Lamb, and by the word of their testimony; and they loved not their lives unto the death.*

The devil is referred to as the accuser of the brethren. That is why he was in the midst, with the angels. That is why he came before God at this time. He wanted to accuse Job and to tell God that Job was not a real man. But we go on to read, "*They overcame him by the blood of the Lamb.*" I love that. "*And by the word of their testimony.*"

"*The blood of the Lamb*" simply means that at the cross Satan received his death wound, for Jesus destroyed the works of the devil by His death. At the cross Satan was virtually dethroned, and now on the basis of Calvary we can depose him in any given meeting if only we know how to claim the victory of Calvary and to plead the efficacy of the blood. Say to the Lord, "You defeated the devil at Calvary, and now I am going to overcome him by the blood You did shed."

Determine to counteract all the moves of the enemy in the ways I have indicated. You know what the cry of Zechariah 3:2 was, "*The* L*ORD* *rebuke thee, O Satan.*" Let us use the same language. May the Holy Spirit help us to exert the influence which is spiritual, not satanic, and heavenly, not merely human.

CHAPTER FIVE:

SUFFERINGS OF THE HOLY SPIRIT

In our study of the Holy Spirit, we have come to the sufferings of the Spirit, and it is our desire in this meditation to classify the treatment of the Holy Spirit, both by the saint and the sinner, in order that we might know how we can please the One about whom we are meditating. The dignity of a person determines more or less the seriousness of a crime committed against him. If you were passing along a street and insulted a pauper, well, perhaps, nothing would be said about it. But if the person happened to be the president of the United States or the king of the British Empire, then the crime would appear to be more serious and punishment would correspond accordingly. The deity of a Person makes any kind of sin against Him awful and egregious. We have been trying to prove from Holy Bible the deity and dignity of the divine Spirit. Therefore, in our present meditation, we are to see how serious any sin is that people may commit against the Holy Spirit.

And let us emphasize this thought in passing, namely, that what one may suffer, the others feel. The three persons in the Godhead are equal. Therefore, what one may suffer the others feel. All the Godhead suffer in the sin of men. Christ is referred to as the arm of the Lord: *"Who hath believed our report? and to whom is the arm of the* L*ORD revealed?"* (Isaiah 53:1). Then, in Luke 11:20, you find our Lord referring to the Holy Spirit as the finger: *"I with the finger of God cast out devils."* By comparing that with another gospel, we know that our Lord had the Holy Spirit in mind.

So, our Lord is the arm, and the Holy Spirit is the finger. My arm is the seat of strength and my finger is the agent of strength, and the strength of my arm is revealed and manifested through these fingers of mine. If a person does not possess fingers, then he cannot very well display the strength of his arm. And so the Lord reveals or manifests His strength as the arm through the Holy Spirit who is the finger. Now if the arm suffers, of course, in like manner, the fingers suffer. If you happen to burn your finger, the pain travels right through that finger up the arm to the head. So what one suffers, all feel.

It is our purpose, then, to classify what the Bible has to say about the sufferings of the Spirit. This may sound a somewhat strange theme, but the more I think of the work of the Spirit, the more I am impressed with the sufferings men and women occasion Him. The Lord Jesus came from heaven and He lived among men for thirty-three years; then He died and His sufferings were over. But have you ever been impressed with this: that the Holy Spirit came from glory on the day of Pentecost and that He has been in the world among sinful men for nearly nineteen hundred years? He has been here all the time since He was bestowed, indwelling men and women and beholding all the sins and the woes of life, and He has tarried here all through that long period.

Let me suggest a threefold division that you can carry with you: there are sufferings caused by sinners; there are sufferings caused by saints and sinners, for these particular sufferings have a double meaning; and then in the last place, there are sufferings caused by saints. Those caused by sinners: the Spirit of God can be blasphemed, spurned, insulted. By saint and sinner: the Spirit of God can be angered, resisted, lied against, tempted. And then by the saints only: the Holy Spirit can be ignored, grieved, quenched.

Now, a word or two regarding these divisions.

I. SUFFERINGS CAUSED BY SINNERS

Let us think of the outstanding sufferings the Holy Spirit endures today, occasioned by the treatment meted out to Him by sinners. And never forget the fact that this is the dispensation of the Spirit of Christ, that we are related very definitely in this age to the Holy Spirit. Now you can take these three aspects if you like, and make them the foundation of the message for your next gospel service, and I feel sure that if you live much in the presence of God that the Holy Spirit will give you a message that will make for the conviction and the regeneration of souls.

1. Sinners can blaspheme the Holy Spirit. Matthew 12:31 says, *"The blasphemy against the Holy Ghost shall not be forgiven unto men."* This aspect of our theme disturbs a good many people. I have come across saints who seemed to fear that they

had committed the unpardonable sin; and I have met sinners who were perturbed because they had caused the Spirit of God to suffer in this way. Now it is not very difficult to understand the teaching of our Lord. He said that they who had spoken against Him would be forgiven, but blasphemy against the Holy Spirit could not be forgiven. By that He meant that the Holy Spirit was to be God's ultimatum. Men could speak against the Savior, but the Savior was going and He said another was coming in the person of the Holy Spirit. And what our Lord really had in mind was this: that if men in this age treat the Holy Spirit as they treated Jesus in His age, then they are without hope, for no one is to come after the Holy Spirit. This is the age of grace—the age or dispensation of the Spirit of grace. So, if men and women in this age treat the Holy Spirit as Jesus was treated in His age, then they shut themselves off from all hope.

And what is blasphemy against the Holy Spirit? Be very careful to tell men and women that the fear they exhibit regarding this sin is evidence that they have not committed it—for persons who reach this stage have no fear at all. They are beyond all feeling and beyond all fear. Thus, the very fear these concerned men and women manifest is evidence that the Spirit of God is still pleading with them and that their hearts are somewhat tender regarding the same. The unpardonable sin, as it is called, is the willful, conscious, final rejection of the Spirit's revelation of Christ. I think that condenses what is at the back of this very terrible sin. The blasphemy against the Holy Spirit is the willful, conscious, final rejection of the Spirit's revelation of the Lord Jesus Christ.

2. We discover that the Holy Spirit can be spurned by sinners. Hebrew 3:7–8 says, "*The Holy Ghost saith, today if ye will hear his voice,* [the voice of the Spirit] *harden not your hearts.*"

Now, we have tried to prove that the Holy Spirit is the direct Agent between the lost soul and the Savior. It is He who convicts the lost soul of its need, and then in the moment of faith, applies the efficacious blood of the Lord Jesus. It is the work of the Holy Spirit to convict the sinner of his need, to illumine his mind regarding his true condition before God. So you will be very careful to point out the awful tendency of this particular sin. As the Holy Spirit says to the sinner, "Today," is the sinner to say in reply, "Not today but tomorrow"? This is a gradual sin; no sinner becomes hard all at once, but through saying no to the Holy Spirit as He speaks time after time, the sinner adds links to the chain that ultimately binds his soul forever.

And you can connect this with Hebrews 6:1–6, which is a portion troubling a good many believers as well as unbelievers, "*...for those who were once enlightened, and have tasted of the heavenly gift, and were made partakers of the Holy Ghost...if they shall fall away, to renew them again unto repentance*" (verses 4, 6). Now, people fall into error and darkness when they persist in applying these conditions to the Christian, making them teach the "falling-away" doctrine. The passage does not describe regenerated people, but souls divinely prepared for the intelligent choice of Christ as Savior. All that you have here is true of believers, but more is necessary to make them believers than you have in this passage.

For example, a believer is one who has not only been enlightened by the Holy Spirit but one who has received the Holy Spirit; and a believer is one who has not only tasted of the heavenly gift but received the heavenly gift. A sinner can be a partaker of the Holy Spirit and yet not be regenerated. Sinners wrought upon by the Holy Spirit partake of His ministry in respect to a mental conception of the truth. The passage describes those whose minds have been illuminated by the Holy Spirit and who have travelled so far on the road and then have receded and trampled underfoot the very truths that the Holy Spirit revealed to them by His power. He can be spurned. You remember how the apostle speaks about those who went out from us but they were not of us. They had the enlightenment of the Spirit, but the day came when they spurned it. And it is impossible to renew such unto repentance.

3. He can be insulted. Hebrews 10:29 says, "*Hath done despite unto the Spirit of grace.*" The word "*despite*" here means insult. Dr. Weymouth has it as insulting the Spirit from whom grace comes. Now, we can shamefully treat or insult the Spirit of grace. This was the sin of Simon Magus, in Acts 8:20, when he insulted the Holy Spirit, believing that the power of the Holy Spirit could be bought with money: "*But Peter said unto him, Thy money perish with thee, because thou hast thought that the gift of God may be purchased with money.*"

How are we going to apply this when we face unconverted men and women? Well, we can tell them that it is a downright insult to the Holy Spirit to say that there is no need for them to be saved today; tomorrow will do. For the Holy Spirit says "today." Then we can also declare this: that the modernist who denies the deity of Christ and the necessity of the cross really despises the Spirit's testimony and insults the Holy Spirit; for the Holy Spirit testifies in the infallible Word to these fundamental themes.

If believers are scorned and insulted, in insulting a child of God we insult the Holy Spirit. That is demonstrated for us, you remember, in the conversion of Saul of Tarsus. He caused those believers to suffer. He was determined to exterminate them, and the Lord revealed Himself to Saul and told him that really, he was persecuting the Lord Himself—not merely His believers. *"I am Jesus whom thou persecutest"* (Acts 9:5). So when a sinner insults a saint of God, he is insulting the Holy Spirit indwelling the saint.

II. SUFFERINGS CAUSED BY SAINTS AND SINNERS

Here you have a group of passages capable of a double application. First of all, both the sinner and the saint can anger the Spirit. The other week, I was in a Bible conference and an outstanding Bible teacher declared that we never have any evidence in the Word of God regarding the wrath of the Spirit, that we read about the wrath of God and we read about the wrath of the Lamb, but we never read about the wrath of the Spirit. And he said the symbol of the Spirit is the dove, and the dove has no gall, and so the Spirit is all love, and He can never show any anger. Well now, if there is love, there is anger; I beg to differ with the teacher in question because in the Word of God, I discover the wrath of the Spirit. If all three in the Godhead are equal, they have equal feelings. Here is Psalm 78:40: *"How oft did they provoke him in the wilderness, and grieve him in the desert!"* Let me give you the translation from the Septuagint: *"They disobeyed and made angry the Spirit of God."* There is very interesting evidence of this in 1 Samuel 11:6, *"The Spirit of God came upon Saul when he heard those tidings, and his anger was kindled greatly."* What is the implication? Why, the Holy Spirit made possible the anger that Saul manifested. The Spirit of God came upon Saul when he heard those tidings, and his anger was kindled greatly. So we can grieve or make angry the Spirit of God.

This is also clearly taught in Isaiah 63:10 (RSV), *"They rebelled and grieved his holy Spirit; therefore he turned to be their enemy, and himself fought against them."* The word for "grieve" there means to make angry. They rebelled and made angry His Spirit, and he turned and became their enemy and fought against them. Thus we do have the wrath of the Spirit.

Let us, therefore, urge sinners to be very careful, lest they rouse the wrath of the Spirit. Let us remind them of Genesis 6:3, "*My spirit shall not always strive with man.*" And may we never forget that this word in Isaiah was spoken of those who professed faith in God. May we never rebel against the Holy Spirit.

2. He can be resisted by sinners and saints. Acts 7:51 says, "*Ye do always resist the Holy Ghost: as your fathers did, so do ye.*" Now, you can use this in the first place when you face the sinner, for we all know what it is to be in gospel meetings where sinners resist the promptings of the Holy Spirit. You have seen them. The Holy Spirit is upon them and they are being operated upon by the Holy Spirit in respect to His ministry of conviction; you feel that they are almost on the verge of receiving Christ, but there they sit and you can see their resistance stamped upon their countenances. It is a very solemn thing to resist the Holy Spirit. They detect His voice and yet deliberately refuse it. We know that active resistance to His gentle persuasion is very serious indeed in the life of a sinner.

But when Stephen uttered this word, he was addressing those who were looked upon as the people of God: "*Ye do always resist the Holy Ghost: as your fathers did*" (Acts 7:51). Add to this the references we quoted in the previous section. Alas, we can resist the Holy Spirit. I wonder if we are conscious of the fact that we have resisted His lordship and sway. Those in the ministry know what it is to be prompted by the Holy Spirit to speak to a soul, and because of timidity you refused to do it, and that opportunity never came again. I remember being deeply impressed with this at one time. The Spirit of God prompted me to speak to a certain person who lived next door to our house. He was a very worldly man and held a prominent position in the high school in the town. One day I was led of the Holy Spirit to speak to that man about eternal things, and I refused. The next day he was brought home dead. And I tremble at the thought that there may be men and women in a lost eternity who might not have been there had I not resisted the Holy Spirit. We know that so often people are led of the Spirit to yield themselves to the work of the Lord in the regions beyond, and refuse, and they live on for the rest of their lives with God's second best.

3. He can be lied against. Acts 5:4 says, "*Thou hast not lied unto men, but unto God.*" Now, here you have an indirect evidence of the deity of the Spirit. Peter told those two people that they had tempted the Spirit of the Lord, and then he goes on to say: "*Thou hast not lied unto men, but unto God.*" The implication is that the Holy Spirit is God. You see, Ananias and Sapphira did not utter a lie—they acted a lie. They pretended to be what they were not, and this is a sin of the sinner as well as of the saint. Oh, we must guard against all secret falsehoods, avoid all deceptive appearances, and flee from false pretenses. It is certainly possible for the sinner to commit this sin. Have you never seen it in a gospel meeting? I have. An unwise evangelist who is more keen about having statistics than the guidance of God regarding his own service may bring a good deal of pressure to bear upon people as he moves among them. And to get rid of him, people say, "Yes, I am saved," yet they have no desire in their hearts at all to come to a definite decision that night. The evangelist goes away, however, and sets another name down as a soul saved. (Even David had to suffer through the sin of counting heads—see 1 Chronicles 21.) And when an unsaved

person declares to an evangelist that the Lord has been taken, when in the heart there has been no transaction, that sinner is lying against the Holy Spirit, and the evangelist, more or less, is responsible for the lie.

And then this can be our sin as saints. We can lie against the Holy Spirit. We can profess that our all is on the altar when, like Ananias and Sapphira, we keep back part of the price. I think we are guilty of this sin more than we realize. Perhaps there is more lying in hymn singing than in any other thing you care to mention. I don't know how you feel, but there are some hymns I am afraid to sing. When I hear a company of people rise and sing very glibly "I surrender all, I surrender all"[6] and then see the way they act and the way they dress, it is a marvel God does not come down and take the tongues out of their throats. I believe if God acted in our day as He acted then with Ananias and Sapphira, there would be a good many empty pews in our churches. I think it is incumbent upon us when we call a congregation to sing a very solemn hymn, to point out something of its solemnity. Rather stand with a closed hymn book than sing something we do not mean and in that way lie against the Holy Spirit.

4. He can be *tempted*. Acts 5:9 says, *"How is it that you have agreed together to tempt the Spirit of the Lord?"* Sometimes a blatant sinner will do that. They say, "Well, if God is God, let Him strike me dead." That is tempting the Spirit of the Lord. We know from history that at times He takes the sinner at his word and proves His power. Ananias and Sapphira thought that the Holy Spirit would wink at their duplicity. They were conscious that they had kept back part of the price. They wanted to be like the other apostles and made the pretense that their all had been

6. Judson W. Van de Venter, "All to Jesus I Surrender," 1896.

given, so they tried an experiment upon the Holy Spirit; they tested His omniscience. Yes, and He knew that they kept back part of the price, and both of them were smitten with sudden death. It is sadly possible to do this, and its solemn significance applies to sinners as well as saints.

III. SUFFERINGS COMMITTED BY SAINTS

Let us now mention one or two things that are related very definitely to us. There are three sufferings that we can cause the Holy Spirit: we can ignore Him; we can grieve Him; we can quench Him.

1. We can *ignore* the Holy Spirit, and that does grieve Him, causing Him a good deal of suffering. Acts 19:2 says, *"Have ye received the Holy Ghost since ye believed?"* and you know the reply of those disciples, *"We have not so much as heard whether there be any Holy Ghost."* How many there are, even in our churches, who are ignorant of the personality of the Holy Spirit.

I remember how a minister friend in Scotland came to me and said, "I would like you to give one or two talks on the Holy Spirit at a convention in our church." And I accepted the invitation. I went back home, and when I sat down and tried to think about the theme, I discovered that I knew very little about the Holy Spirit. I was convicted of my ignorance and of my limitations in that respect, and when the convention was over, I determined to know all I could about this Marvelous One. And I can tell you that my whole life and ministry were marvelously helped and changed as a result of that study.

Yes, we can ignore the Holy Spirit. The New Testament ideal for the Christian is the constant recognition of the personality of the Spirit and the daily enthronement of the Spirit over the life. Ignorance is a sin in a saved person. This aspect has to do with my deeper knowledge of the Word of God, for if I am ignorant of the truth of the Spirit, I shall be ignorant of the contents of that blessed Word. We can ignore Him. I wonder if anyone who reads this has ignored the Spirit. If so, let there come correction. We can all study this truth and get to realize something of the personality and the deity of the Spirit. And such a revelation may come as a second conversion.

2. We can *grieve* Him. Ephesians 4:30 says, "*Grieve not the holy Spirit of God.*" Now, remember when you are dealing with this, if you are going to pass it on to believers, the grieving of the Spirit does not affect the sealing. I have heard some suggest that if we grieve the Holy Spirit, we can break the seal, and He will depart from us. Impossible! What God does is forever, and when the Holy Spirit as the seal enters, nothing and no one can break the seal. The grieving does not affect the sealing. We are sealed, says the apostle, unto the day of redemption. How can we grieve the Spirit? This is our sin as sealed ones.

Where do you think Ephesians 4:30 comes in? It comes in between verses 29 and 31. "Well," you say, "where else would it come?" Well now, if you read verse 29 and then verse 31 on the other side, you can find out what does grieve the Holy Spirit. You have a marvelous sermon there, right in the context. Verse 29: unprofitable talk grieves the Spirit—light, frivolous, unspiritual conversation. Then, when you pass on to verse 30 and come to verse 31, you will find that all un-Christlike actions grieve the Holy Spirit. Unprofitable talk is on the one side and un-Christlike actions are on the other.

Here is a very striking thing: This word "grieve" is a Gethsemane word. If you turn back to Matthew 26:37, you will remember Jesus "*began to be sorrowful.*" Oh, may we ever live to please the Spirit. May we be more sensitive regarding His feelings. Grieving is my sin as a saint. If I permit that which grieves Him, it will affect my communion and growth in holiness and sanctification, inward and outward and upward.

3. We can *quench* the Spirit. 1 Thessalonians 5:19 says, *"Quench not the Spirit."* Now this word *quench* really means "put out the fire," and so we are to be careful lest we put out the fire of the Spirit. Note that I do not mean that we have the power to put out the Spirit from our lives but rather, that we have the power to put out the fire of the Spirit. We can dampen His power if we are not very careful.

Here again, we have a great help if we look at the narrative. How can we quench the Holy Spirit? If you read on in 1 Thessalonians 5, verses 20–22 explain how it is possible for the saint to quench the Holy Spirit.

Verse 20 says, *"Despise not prophesyings,"* and the word there means "preaching." So if we fail to be responsive to the blessed Word, by our lack of response we quench the Spirit and put out the fire.

Verse 21, *"Prove all things; hold fast that which is good."* If in these apostate days, we fail to try or test the spirits whether they be of God, then because of the lack of spiritual discernment we quench the Spirit.

Then in verse 22, *"Abstain from all appearance of evil."* Not only evil, but also the appearance of it; and if we fail to abstain from the very appearance of evil, then we quench the Spirit.

And this putting out the fire or quenching the Spirit operates in a twofold way:

I can quench the fire in other hearts. That is the implication here, I think. Have you never seen the fire quenched in a young convert? I have. He has stood, and in all his humility he has confessed Christ, possibly for the first time, and an old saint has come along and criticized him for the way in which he expressed himself; and that young convert never opened his lips again. We can quench the fire of the Spirit in others by criticism, by jealousy, by unkindness, by the lack of consideration.

Then we can quench the fire in our own hearts, extinguish the flame of the Spirit by sin and disobedience and worldly desires. I may be speaking to a preacher or teacher or Christian worker in whom the fire was once bright, but in place of the fire nothing but ashes. You have lost your vision, your passion, and your enthusiasm. You know what happened? Why is the fire not as fierce as it used to be? Thank God, the Holy Spirit is still with you. Once you deliberately exterminate from your life those things that quench the fire of the Spirit, then He will reveal Himself again and the old flame and passion will be yours.

Quenching is the sin of a servant and has to do with service, either with my own service or with the service of others.

CHAPTER SIX:

SEVENFOLD MANIFESTATION OF THE HOLY SPIRIT

In Revelation 1:4, you have a very descriptive phrase "*the seven Spirits.*" The Hebrew significance of seven is that of abundance. It carries with it the idea of perfection. Applied to the Spirit of God, the number indicates the plenitude of His power and also His diversified activity; it describes the fullness of spiritual activity in respect to the work of the Spirit of God.

Kindly note the plenitude of the Spirit's power and His diversified activity as you think of the way in which He is revealed in the Word of God. You know how this figure seven is related to the Holy Spirit in the book of Revelation. Four times over, He is referred to as the seven Spirits of God, which, of course, indicates that all His fullness is derived from God, the seven Spirits *of* God. Then He is referred to in chapter 4, verse 5 as the seven lamps of fire burning before the throne. There you have the fullness of His governmental action. As the seven lamps of fire, He has the power to search out and expose everything that is alien to His holy mind and will.

Then in Revelation 5:6, He is referred to as the seven horns. Horn, in the Word of God, is the symbol of power. So here you have the fullness of His strength or power manifested in the execution of judgment.

Also in Revelation 5:6 (RSV), you have this very arresting phrase, *"with seven eyes."* This implies that the Holy Spirit possesses the perfection of intelligence. He has the power to reveal, and the power to destroy. Full of eyes, He can penetrate; and being seven lamps, He can reveal; and being seven horns, He can destroy all that is revealed by His power. If you apply the number to our Lord, you can easily see how there was the sevenfold manifestation of the Spirit's operation in the life and work of our Lord.

In Isaiah 11:2 you find that the Holy Spirit is referred to as working upon our Lord in a sevenfold way—as the Spirit of the Lord resting upon Him, as the Spirit of wisdom, as the Spirit of understanding, as the Spirit of counsel, as the Spirit of might, as the Spirit of knowledge, and as the Spirit of the fear of the Lord. As a prism reveals all the colors in the light, so here you have the sevenfold manifestation of the Spirit's work in the life of our Lord.

You have the same thing again in Isaiah 61:1–2. Our Lord laid hold of this old prophecy and related it to Himself. He was enabled to do seven things by the operation of the Spirit: 1) preach good tidings unto the meek; 2) bind up the brokenhearted; 3) proclaim liberty to the captives; 4) and the opening of the prison to them that are bound; 5) proclaim the acceptable year of the Lord 6) and the day of vengeance of our God; and 7) comfort all that mourn.

If you are giving a message, you could here have another word on the sevenfold work or the sevenfold relationship of the Spirit of God to the church of God. You can speak of the diversity of His gifts and of the way in which all those gifts are united. Of course, you will dwell upon 1 Corinthians 12, where the gifts of the Spirit are united and then you will use a passage like Ephesians 4:3–6, where you have the seven unities of the Spirit to be kept: one body, one spirit, one hope of your calling, one Lord, one faith, one baptism, one God and Father of all.

But in this message we are to think of the sevenfold manifestation of the Spirit in respect to the believer. Now, confusion, blunder, and sorrow are ours if we fail to mark the difference between the manifestations of the Spirit. Some are initial and final; others are initial and continuous. There are seven things that we desire to emphasize about the Holy Spirit: the baptism, the gift, the indwelling, the anointing, the sealing, the earnest, and the filling.

THE BAPTISM

Allow me to say that that phrase in itself is not a scriptural one. The Bible nowhere speaks about the baptism of the Holy Spirit. There is a good deal said about the baptism in or baptism with the Holy Spirit. It is very essential to understand what the New Testament means when it refers to the baptism with the Holy Spirit. The baptism with the Holy Spirit is not the same as the infilling of the Holy Spirit. We must not identify this with what some believers refer to as a second blessing.

There are seven passages in all relating to the baptism with the Spirit, four in the Gospels, Matthew 3:11; Mark 1:8; Luke 3:16; and John 1:26, 33. Then you have two references in the book of Acts: 1:5 and 11:16. And finally, you have one in the Epistles: 1 Corinthians 12:13. Now, suppose you bring all these references together, what do you discover? Well, those in the Gospels point forward to a focal point, and the remaining references in the Acts and in 1 Corinthians point back to some focal point. And we believe that that focal point was Pentecost, and that baptism with the Holy Spirit was that coming of the Holy Spirit whereby the mystical body was instituted. That is borne out, I think, in 1 Corinthians 12:13 (RSV), *"By one Spirit we were all baptized into one body."*

So, as I have indicated, this manifestation is initial and final. The Lord Jesus, according to His own word in the Gospels, is the Baptizer. And, as you can see, by this baptism we are placed into an element. By the filling, or the infilling, the element is placed within us. That brings us to the word that Dr. Scofield has, "one baptism, many fillings or infillings." Baptism is a beginning. It stands for the beginning of our Christian experience. It is the primary beginning of regeneration as we have indicated, the initial work of regeneration. And so in our experience, the baptism with the Holy Spirit is equivalent to regeneration, when, through the acceptance of the Lord Jesus we are made part of that mystical body known as His church. If this is true and the baptism with the Holy Spirit is the initial and final work of the Spirit of God in the hour of regeneration, why ask the Lord to do something that has already been accomplished?

THE GIFT

In the next place, we have what is referred to as the gift of the Spirit. In Acts 2:38, there is a distinct reference to this gift, *"Then Peter said unto them, Repent, and be baptized every one of you in the name of Jesus Christ for the remission of sins, and ye shall receive the gift of the Holy Ghost."* Now, this is linked on to the last aspect. There is a similarity between the baptism with the Holy Spirit and the gift of the Spirit; and here again, this aspect is initial and final.

You will remember that we have already pointed out that we could never receive any more of a person than that person. So if the Holy Spirit is a person (and we know Him to be from the Word of God not only a person but a divine Person), then we can never have any more of the Holy Spirit as a person than the person Himself; which means that when He enters, He enters in His totality as a person. You can never receive personality by installments. So, in the hour of faith, the believing sinner receives the Holy Spirit as the gift of the ascended Lord.

The realization of the presence of the Holy Spirit within may be almost akin to the joy of receiving the Lord Jesus. We have known believers who knew all about the finished work of the Lord Jesus but who were ignorant of the truth of the Holy Spirit. Then, in a conference meeting or a gathering for the deepening of the spiritual life, the truth of the Holy Spirit was emphasized and the realization and recognition of the fact that the Holy Spirit was within as the source of power and victory brought an experience of joy that they had not known in the hour of regeneration.

But although a believer may be ignorant of the fact that the Holy Spirit is within, nevertheless He is within. *"If any man have not the Spirit of Christ, he is none of his"* (Romans 8:9). Therefore, it is not right for believers to ask the Lord for the Holy Spirit. No need for believers to have tarrying meetings to ask God for the Holy Spirit. They would never have been Christians had it not been for the entrance of the Holy Spirit. You may say, "What about Luke 11:13, where our Lord said to those around Him, *'If you, then, who are evil, know how to give good gifts to your children, how much more will the heavenly Father give the Holy Spirit to those who ask Him!'* (RSV)?" I would reply that that verse was uttered before Pentecost, and we have no record that those disciples as a body asked the Lord for the Holy Spirit. It was Jesus Himself who asked the Father for the Holy Spirit that the same might be the possession of His people. John 14:16 says, *"I will pray the Father, and he shall give you another Comforter."*

I think there is a good deal of wrong teaching about Pentecost. We are not exhorted in these days to wait as the apostles waited, for the coming of the Holy Spirit. The waiting on the part of those disciples was not a condition for the reception of the Holy Spirit. The Holy Spirit could not descend until the Lord Jesus was glorified. The moment He ascended and seated Himself at the Father's right hand, the Holy Spirit came according to the promise of the Father. When the day of Pentecost was fully come and the disciples were gathered together in the upper chamber, then, according to divine promise, the Holy Spirit descended upon those waiting souls. Let us not insult God by asking for something, nay, *Someone* already bestowed.

THE INDWELLING

First Corinthians 3:16 says, *"Know ye not that ye are the temple of God, and that the Spirit of God dwelleth in you?"* Here you have a manifestation of the Spirit that is initial and continuous. This has to do with our continuous security. The gift of the Spirit indicates the entrance of the One who regenerates. Here you have the means whereby we are kept: *"Blessed be the God and Father of our Lord Jesus Christ, which according to his abundant mercy hath begotten us again unto a lively hope by the resurrection of Jesus Christ from the dead"* (1 Peter 1:3). It is very necessary to emphasize this truth, that when the Holy Spirit enters, He enters to remain. He is the tenant who can never be ejected. No matter what the child of God may be capable of, the Holy Spirit can never be thrust from the heart and life. We may lose the consciousness of His presence as the result of our sin, but the consciousness of His presence and the reality of His indwelling are two different things altogether.

There are a good many believers who live under a cloud. They seem to think that because of some act of disobedience, the Holy Spirit has departed from them, and they hark back to Psalm 51:11, *"Take not thy holy spirit from me."* But remember the distinction between the dispensations. David lived in the old dispensation, when there was not the full revelation regarding the personality of the Holy Spirit. In the Old Testament, the Holy Spirit is treated more as a power than as a person. And as a power, He came upon persons that they might accomplish some specific work. And the implication is that when the work was accomplished, the Spirit as a power was withdrawn. In that respect David cried, *"Take not thy holy spirit from me."* As the anointed king, he required continual power. But as I have said, that passage is related to the old dispensation. No believer in this dispensation of the Spirit has any right to say, *"Take not thy holy spirit from me"*; for God will never take from a believer what

He has given to that believer. So when He enters, He enters to remain.

It would make all the difference in our life and ministry if only we recognized and revered the Holy Spirit's indwelling. If only we carried about with us this solemn thought—that we form the temple of the Holy Spirit. If only we could refer everything to the Spirit of God, realizing that He indwells us, and turn to Him no matter what the difficulty or the occasion may be, for guidance, advice, and direction, just as we turn to a friend whose face we see. Brethren, the recognition of the indwelling of the Holy Spirit makes for power in life and fruitfulness in service.

THE ANOINTING

"He which…hath anointed us, is God" (2 Corinthians 1:21). There are one or two passages that you must bring together and use under this section. For example, there is 1 John 2:20: *"But ye have an unction from the Holy One, and ye know all things"* and verse 27: *"But the anointing which ye have received of him abideth in you, and ye need not that any man teach you: but as the same anointing teacheth you of all things, and is truth, and is no lie, and even as it hath taught you, ye shall abide in him."* Then you have passages suggesting that God Himself is the Anointer. The Holy Spirit is the anointing; the Father is the Anointer. Then Acts 10:38, where, in reference to our Lord's ministry, we read that *"God anointed Jesus of Nazareth with the Holy Ghost and with power."* Now, our Lord was anointed not *by* the Holy Spirit but *with* the Holy Spirit. The Spirit came upon Him from the Father, the Anointer, after the anointing. So the anointing is not a blessing; it is not merely a gift or a grace. The anointing is

the Person in all His fullness, resting upon us, energizing us to accomplish a divine task.

Have we been brought to the place where, like the Savior, we have received the anointing with the Spirit for service? Although our Lord was born of the Spirit and through those first thirty years in His humble home at Nazareth was justified or vindicated by the Spirit, yet when He stepped out into His ministry of three and a half years, He received a distinct anointing with the Spirit, that He might be empowered for the activities awaiting Him. Now, this experience is initial and continuous. The anointing stands for our complete separation unto God for the fulfillment of His divine plan for our individual life.

In the Old Testament, everything and everybody touched by oil was given to God. So at Jordan, by the anointing with the Spirit, the Lord, in a very peculiar sense, was separated unto God for that marvelous ministry of His, lasting only for three and a half years. And in secret, the Holy Spirit for thirty years was preparing Jesus for that ministry of three and a half years. Let us remember that if God is taking pains with us, as we face some particular task in life, we have every right to ask the Lord for this unction of the Holy One. May we ever be delivered from facing solemn tasks without seeking the anointing with the Spirit! We may be brought to a crisis when, very deliberately, we will seek the anointing with the Spirit. But the anointing is not only initial, it is continuous. And as we go out and go through our ministry and find ourselves up against crises where we require peculiar power, wisdom, understanding, and guidance, if we look to the Lord in this way, the Holy Spirit will undertake for us and come upon us in a way that will make us efficient.

Now, at this point, I can answer one of the questions often asked. "If the Holy Spirit is always with us and always in us, how can He come upon us? Does this not suggest that He leaves us, so that He may come upon us?" He is ever within us as a person, but at times He comes upon us as the power of God. And then remember that the Holy Spirit, although He is present in the life, is also omnipresent. He is not only within us, He is around us. You see, the air is within me and the air is around me. I have the air resting upon me and I have the air within me. So, although the Holy Spirit is within as a person, because He is omnipresent and fills all space, He can come upon us if we are brought to some crisis in our ministry requiring unusual power and heavenly wisdom.

THE SEALING

"And grieve not the holy Spirit of God, whereby ye are sealed unto the day of redemption" (Ephesians 4:30). The sealing of the Holy Spirit is the evidence that we are regenerated. In this verse is the key word that we use under this aspect. Here the apostle tells us that we are not to grieve the Holy Spirit of God, whereby we are sealed unto the day of redemption.

Look at your concordance, and gather together all the references in the Word of God where you find the word "seal." You will then have a good deal of information when you come to give a message on the Holy Spirit as the Seal. God is the Sealer and the Holy Spirit is the Seal. Believers, of course, are the sealed ones. And, as I have said, this also is both initial and final. Once sealed, we are sealed forever. A good many years ago, in the Keswick Convention in Britain, I heard a teacher say that if believers were not very careful, they could break the seal. That, I affirm, is not true to Holy Bible. For the seal is not something; the seal is Someone. The Holy Spirit is the Seal, and He cannot be broken. He cannot be destroyed, and He can never be thrust from the life into which He has entered. He dwells within forever.

Let us classify the passages dealing with the seal. Immediately, of course, we remember Jeremiah 32:9–10, where Hanameel bought the field and then sealed it:

> *And I bought the field of Hanameel my uncle's son, that was in Anathoth, and weighed him the money, even seventeen shekels of silver. And I subscribed the evidence, and sealed it, and took witnesses, and weighed him the money in the balances.*

There the seal indicates a finished transaction. The field was bought and then it was sealed. So the Holy Spirit as the Seal is the evidence of the finished work on the cross. I know that Jesus died at Calvary. I know that Jesus rose again. I know that Jesus ascended. I know that Jesus is at the right hand of the Father, for the Holy Spirit is here. He is the Seal of the finished work of the cross. And, of course, being within our hearts, we know that we are eternally secure, sealed unto the day of redemption. That, of course, implies the redemption of the body. We have a redeemed spirit in an old body. But this body, this old natural life, limits the activities of the redeemed spirit within. One day, however, we are to have the body that corresponds to the new life within; so we wait for the redemption of the body. And the Holy Spirit is the Seal of this completed transaction.

Then you will find that a seal indicates security as well as a finished transaction. In Esther 8:8, the queen received the decree from the king. And we read that it was sealed with the king's ring. It was secure: "*Write ye also for the Jews, as it liketh you, in the king's name, and seal it with the king's ring: for the writing which is written in the king's name, and sealed with the king's ring, may no man reverse.*"

You have the same thought in Daniel 6:17, where they placed a seal upon the lion's den, sealed with the king's seal: "*And a stone was brought, and laid upon the mouth of the den; and the king sealed it with his own signet, and with the signet of his lords; that the purpose might not be changed concerning Daniel.*"

And so the Holy Spirit within is the evidence of my security. I know that I cannot be lost for the Holy Spirit is within. If it is possible for the Holy Spirit to leave me, then it is possible for believers to un-regenerate themselves, But once a son, a son forever, and the Holy Spirit within is the token of my security.

In the next place, there is the idea of ownership; you will find that in Jeremiah 32:11–12, where the seal speaks of ownership:

> *So I took the evidence of the purchase, both that which was sealed according to the law and custom, and that which was open: And I gave the evidence of the purchase unto Baruch the son of Neriah, the son of Maaseiah, in the sight of Hanameel mine uncle's son, and in the presence of the witnesses that subscribed the book of the purchase, before all the Jews that sat in the court of the prison.*

When the apostle in Ephesians 4:30 refers to the Spirit of God as the seal, he knew what he was talking about, and he was applying something to those Ephesians they would readily understand. Ephesus was a maritime city, having an extensive trade in timber. And the ship masters would purchase a good quantity of timber, stamp their seal upon it, and then, of course, send their servants to secure their property. As the ship master sealed his timber and by the seal indicated that such was his own, the Holy Spirit within us is the seal, the evidence of divine ownership.

THE EARNEST

> *Who hath also sealed us, and given the earnest of the Spirit in our hearts.* (2 Corinthians 1:22)

> *Now he that hath wrought us for the selfsame thing is God, who also hath given unto us the earnest of the Spirit.* (2 Corinthians 5:5)

The earnest of the Spirit is initial and final. The Holy Spirit is the earnest; none of His gifts can be looked upon as the earnest. He, Himself, is the earnest and He is within our hearts as such. He is referred to as the earnest three times over in the above references. This New Testament word "earnest" is equivalent to the Old Testament word "pledge."

A good many years ago, when in Scotland, I was interested to find that the Scots have an old Scottish word that expresses very forcibly this New Testament word "*earnest.*" They have the word *arles*. If a farmer wants land and goes out and buys a few acres, after looking at the estate and completing the transaction, he takes what they call the *arles*. He has a little spade, and taking a quantity of the earth, a part of the ground that he has purchased, he will put that earth in a sack, and that is the arles.

That is the earnest; that is the pledge that all the rest belongs to him.

Now the Holy Spirit is within as the earnest. What does that mean? Why, that He is the pledge of our full and final redemption. As that little quantity of earth tells the farmer that all the rest he has purchased belongs to him, so the Holy Spirit within my heart is the pledge, or the earnest, or the arles that all that God has provided for me will ultimately be mine.

THE FILLING

"Be filled with the Spirit" (Ephesians 5:18). Here we come to the source of grace for all our needs. This is initial and continuous. There are two words that we must bear in mind when we think of this last aspect of our theme. There is the word *filled* and then the word *full,* and you will find yourself in a good deal of doubt and misapprehension when you come to study the Acts and the Epistles if you do not distinguish between these two words, *filled* and *full.*

Filled, when it is used in respect to the Holy Spirit, indicates His intermittent work, something that is casual or spasmodic. For example, in the Old Testament, we read that Bezaleel was filled with the Spirit. Well, he was appointed to do something very particular in respect to the erection of the tabernacle, and so for a specific work he received this unique unction of the Spirit of God. When his work was accomplished, then the power of the Spirit was withdrawn. We read that the Virgin Mary was filled with the Holy Spirit for something very solemn and wonderful, namely, the conception of our blessed Lord. So, when we have any special need, there may be experienced the special filling or infilling of the Holy Spirit.

But then there is the word *full*. We read that Stephen was full of the Holy Spirit. We read that Jesus was full of the Holy Spirit. Here you have a normal experience—something not spasmodic or intermittent but habitual. And this is the way in which the apostle in Ephesians 5:18 uses the word when he writes, "*Be filled with the Spirit*." It really means, "Be filled full." And the idea is that of an experience that is normal.

Beloved, this experience ought to be a normal one. Here is a command, not to *do* something, but a command to *allow* something to be accomplished within our own lives. The word carries with it the idea of passive attitude. If we think of the Holy Spirit as something—as a kind of mysterious influence or power we must possess, then our attitude will be an active one, and we are always reaching out after some power God has for us. But if we believe that the Spirit of God is a person, then our attitude is a passive one; and this verse is in the passive sense. We yield ourselves unto the Lord that He might make possible this normal experience. Yes, this precept in Ephesians 5:18 is not for a crisis but indicates the whole habit of the Christian life. I wonder if we can truthfully say that we are full of the Spirit. Do we allow the Holy Spirit to rise as the well of water and fill and permeate and dominate every part of our life within? Be ye infilled with the Spirit. Let the fullness of the Spirit be your normal experience. Oh, may God give us grace to possess our possession!

A few years ago, in one of our London papers, there was a very striking story told of a man who took ill on a London street and who was carried away to the Bethnal Green Infirmary. He died, and at the inquest, it was discovered that he was a comparatively rich man, for he had just handed over to his brother twenty thousand dollars, and had sold shares to the value of something like fifteen hundred. Yet he lived in one room, we are told, for which he paid just one dollar a week. He was only sixty years of age; he looked eighty. He was dressed in rags and tatters, and he used to walk the streets of London picking up pieces of stale bread. The verdict of the jury was (and it was this that impressed me), that he "died of self-starvation, when he had ample funds in his possession, and a banking account."

God save us from spiritual starvation when we have the vast resources of the Holy Spirit at our disposal!

CHAPTER SEVEN:

THE HOLY SPIRIT AS FIRE

There are many symbols used in the Word of God descriptive of the manifold operations of the Spirit. Most symbols are drawn from animate and inanimate objects, thus opening up a wonderful field of study to those who want to apply the truth of the Spirit. I suggest to you that you commence a study on the symbols of the Holy Spirit. Let me try to give you one or two helpful hints that you can apply to other symbols as you meet them in the course of your study of the Spirit. All the emblems taken together are necessary to express and illustrate the person and the work of the Holy Spirit. One of the most common symbols is that of fire. Fire is used in four ways when it comes to the power of the Spirit. First, fire is used to describe the purifying power of the Spirit. Isaiah 4:4 says, *"When the Lord shall have washed away the filth of the daughters of Zion, and shall have purged the blood of Jerusalem from the midst thereof by the spirit of judgment, and by the spirit of burning.*" If I were taking a basic verse for a study on this symbol, I would lay hold of Isaiah 4:4, "*the spirit of burning.*" As you meditate upon this verse, remember that as the Spirit of judgment, the Holy Spirit condemns filth; and as the Spirit of burning, He consumes the filth.

Second, this fire is also descriptive of the consuming power of the Spirit.

> *He shall baptize you with the Holy Ghost, and with fire; whose fan is in his hand, and he will thoroughly purge his floor, and gather his wheat into the garner; but he will burn up the chaff with unquenchable fire.* (Matthew 2:11–12)

There are a good many believers who stumble over this passage. Thus they pray for what they call "the baptism of fire," and they tell us that fire is something distinct here from the Holy Spirit. I suggest that the Holy Spirit is the fire and that we can interpret the passage, "He shall baptize you with the Holy Ghost, who is fire." The consuming power of the Spirit is in the mind of our Lord. The judgment aspect of the Spirit is here emphasized by the Master.

Third, fire is descriptive of the *energizing* power of the Spirit. Acts 2:3 says, "*There appeared unto them cloven tongues like as of fire, and it sat upon each of them.*" You will note that a separate flame rested upon each disciple, and that indicates, I think, the bestowal of individual gifts for service and the power to exercise those personal gifts.

Fourth, fire is used to describe the illuminating power of the Spirit. Revelation 4:5 says, "*And there were seven lamps of fire burning before the throne, which are the seven Spirits of God.*"

And this term indicates the Spirit's power to penetrate and illuminate. Seven is one of the perfect numbers of Holy Bible. And so here you have a symbol describing the perfect light and radiance of the Spirit of God.

Now, coming to the theme proper and analyzing what the Bible has to say about fire, we have this outline before us. You may want to know how to gather your material together. Well, this is the method I adopt. Suppose, now, we think of the symbol before us—the Holy Spirit as fire. With a concordance in hand, we look at all the references containing the word "fire." And then we make our selection and our application accordingly. If you use the dove as a symbol of the Holy Spirit, look at all the references in the Word of God where you find the dove mentioned, and then make your selection and application accordingly. You have a wonderful wealth of material in the Bible itself.

FIRE WARMS

First of all, then, we discover from the Word of God, that fire warms: "*I am warm, I have seen the fire*" (Isaiah 44:16). This passage suggests a cold wintry day and the cheerful, warming effect of a glowing fire. You come indoors and you are cold and numb, and you sit before a blazing fire, and as you sit in the presence of the fire you are warmed.

We live too much in spiritual winter; we need the divine fire to warm our cold hearts. This is the great need of today, I think, in church life and service. We have plenty of coals and wood; the fire is well laid; organization is perfect in every detail. But what is the use of a well-laid fire unless you apply the match and turn the well-laid fire into a blaze?

And what we sadly need today is the fiery flame of the Holy Spirit. Fire warms. There is the absence of love for souls, zeal in service, fervor in prayer, devotion, and consecration, the blaze of atmosphere, sacrifice in worship, and the igniting power of influence. We are not set on fire for God. We need this fiery work of the Spirit. Fire warms. A Chinese convert was asked what he thought China's greatest need was, and he replied, "Give us men and women with hot hearts, who can tell the story of Jesus." And the world needs burning hearts. I wonder if we are on fire for God.

Thy Holy Spirit, Lord, alone,
Can deeper love inspire;
His power alone within our souls
Can light the sacred fire.[7]

We know, do we not, that a tepid, lukewarm condition is abhorrent to God? *"Because thou art lukewarm, and neither cold nor hot, I will spue thee out of my mouth"* (Revelation 3:16). Oh, for the fire that warms. It is a matter of fire or freeze. If we are not blazing, then we are freezing. Now, it seems to me that we need this aspect of the Spirit's work to banish the cold that has settled upon the church today. And let us beware of the strange fire that many offer. There is a good deal of strange fire in the organized church today, but we want the real fire, even the fire that warms.

FIRE SPREADS

Who maketh his angels spirits; his ministers a flaming fire. (Psalm 104:4)

7. Fanny Crosby, "Thy Holy Spirit, Lord, Alone," 1885.

> *The fire hath devoured the pastures of the wilderness, and the flame hath burned all the trees of the field.* (Joel 1:19)

The igniting power of fire is indeed terrible. Fire spreads with a remarkable rapidity. You know what they do in forests or prairies when fire breaks out: they make huge gaps in order to stay the course of the fiery flame. The late Dr. Torrey, in a message on the Holy Spirit, used to tell the story of the great fire of Chicago in 1872. That fire was started as a woman was milking a cow. She was sitting there in the barn milking the cow by the light of a lamp that was somewhat dim, and the cow kicked the lantern over and the straw caught fire, and then the barn was enveloped with flames and so the fire spread until the main part of Chicago, a mile wide and three miles long, was covered with flames. Only two buildings were left standing after that great fire. Fire spreads.

Oh, the power of one little flame, lit by the Holy Spirit in the bosom of the humblest! We think of what happened on the day of Pentecost. Peter, before Pentecost, was afraid to confess his Lord before a servant girl; and yet on the day of Pentecost, the Holy Spirit came upon him as fire, and because fire spreads, through the simple testimony he gave, three thousand were brought to the feet of the Crucified. You can apply that in many ways. You can think of a missionary leaving the homeland and going to the regions beyond and living out his life there, and ultimately gathering around himself multitudes who have learned to love the Savior through his instrumentality. But, alas, we are destitute of the contagious igniting, spreading power of the Holy Spirit. We need tongues of fire and hearts of love to preach the reconciling word. I wonder if others are being enthused as they come into contact with our lives.

FIRE ILLUMINATES

The shining of a flaming fire by night. (Isaiah 4:5)

He led them with a cloud and all the night with a light of fire. (Psalm 78:14)

He was a burning and a shining light. (John 5:35)

He, John the Baptist, was that lamp, burning and shining. Now, burning can stand for enthusiasm and deep spiritual experience. Shining can stand for knowledge and wisdom and intellect. I am glad that the burning comes first; experience before education. Where the two are combined, you have twin sisters. But of the two, let us have men of experience, men who know God, men who know something of the indwelling power of the Spirit of God, men who have hot hearts to preach the love of Jesus. John was first of all a burning light. Then he was a shining light. Now, fire illuminates. All of us are cognizant of the illuminating power of the Spirit of God. As the Spirit of light, the Holy Spirit operates in a threefold way. He throws light upon the Word; then He throws light upon our path, illuminating a good many things in life; and then He throws light upon sin. A word or two regarding each of these:

First, He throws light upon the Word. It is the prerogative of the divine Spirit to illumine the Word He has inspired. That is why He is called the Spirit of wisdom and revelation, and the Spirit of truth; for He it is who has the power to open our eyes that we may behold wondrous things out of God's law. All that we need is within God's law, but we need the illumination of the Holy Spirit in order to discover these things. Sometimes you stumble across a certain truth and you say, "Well, I never saw that in the Bible before." But it was there all the time. What happened was simply this: through the gracious influence of the Holy Spirit, your eyes were opened to see that very thing in the sacred Scriptures. So the Holy Spirit illuminates the Word. He is the interpreter of the Word.

The story is told of a student of Dante who could not understand the work of that greatest poet of the dead. He went with Dante's book to Dante's tomb and got down on his knees, opened the work of Dante, and cried, "Master, light, more light, still more light." Dante did not rise from the grave and interpret his work. But the humblest child of God can bow before the Spirit of God and say, "Light, more light, still more light," and the Holy Spirit who inspired the Word can interpret the Word to the humblest believer. Revelation is not a matter of education. Revelation comes directly from the Holy Spirit of God.

Second, He throws light upon our path. If we are beset with problems and difficulties in life and service, we have an infallible guide in the Holy Spirit.

Third, He reveals sin. He throws light into the darkest cells, and we have no need to be afraid of the illuminating power of the Holy Spirit in this respect, for what the light reveals, the precious blood can cleanse.

FIRE CONSUMES

> *And there rose up fire out of the rock and consumed the flesh and the unleavened cakes.* (Judges 6:21)

> *For our God is a consuming fire.* (Hebrews 12:29)

There burns within the heart of the Spirit a divine hatred for sin. Fire is expressive of the divine judgment upon sin. I was very interested, one day, in studying this theme, to discover that all through the Word of God, fire is related to all the judgments that are outlined.

For example, take the unsaved. Second Thessalonians 1:7–8 says, "*The Lord Jesus shall be revealed from heaven with his mighty angels, in flaming fire taking vengeance on them that know not God, and that obey not the gospel of our Lord Jesus Christ.*" Then fire is related to the judgment of the deceived nations. Revelation 20:9 says, "*Fire came down from God out of heaven, and devoured them.*" The fire is connected with the judgment of God upon the heavens and the earth, upon the heavens, these aerial heavens, for they form the abode of Satan and his wicked hosts. He is the prince of the power of the air, and so the heavens are polluted in the sight of God. Judgment is to fall upon the earth because of the curse pronounced upon sin and because this earth bears the stain of our Redeemer's blood. "*But the heavens and the earth, which are now, by the same word are kept in store, reserved unto fire against the day of judgment and perdition of ungodly men*" (2 Peter 3:7). Fire is also connected with the judgment of God upon Satan and lost souls. In Revelation 20:10–15, the devil was cast into the lake of fire, and "*whosoever was not found written in the book of life was cast into the lake of fire*" (verse 15).

In the last place (and this ought to cause us to tremble, seeing that we are Christian workers), fire is associated with the judgment of the Lord upon the works of Christians. First Corinthians 3:13 says, "*The fire shall try every man's work, of what sort it is.*" Then the wood and the hay and the stubble in service are to be consumed. May we allow the Holy Spirit, who is fire, to consume the wood and the hay and the stubble now, so that when we stand before the Lord at the judgment seat, we may have nothing but the gold and the silver and the precious stones. Yes, the Holy Spirit as fire is waiting to consume everything that is antagonistic to His holy mind and will. He waits to burn up all the dross of pride, the rags of selfishness, the failure of unholy desires, the chaff of useless endeavor. Oh, to let pride of every sort be consumed by the Holy Spirit who is fire! In Isaiah 3:24 there is a very interesting phrase. The prophet speaks of "*burning instead of beauty.*" And I know that this is our personal prayer: that all false pride, false beauty, all there is of the self-life, that which belongs to the flesh and the world, might be consumed by the fiery flame of the Spirit of God.

May He give us burning in the place of false beauty!

FIRE SOFTENS

For God maketh my heart soft. (Job 23:16)

This is a wonderful expression. The difficulty is that we are too hard for God to use. We do not know the mellowing, softening power of the Spirit of God. Not so long ago, in a certain English town, while having a few special services, I stayed with a doctor and his wife. The lady was a converted woman, but the doctor was not a Christian. One day the wife said to me, "I wish you would join me in prayer for my husband. I long to see him saved. If you have a fitting opportunity, you might speak to him about these eternal things." After living with that woman for two or three days, I could see why her husband was not being won for the Lord. She had a hard, cold, unsympathetic nature. There was a lack of the sympathy for unconverted men and women that the deep love of the Holy Spirit makes possible.

And I felt that if only she had known something of the softening influence of the Spirit of God, her husband would have been a Christian.

Now, fire softens. A very fitting illustration is the steelworks: here is the cold, hard iron, and it is plunged into the fiery furnace, from there it runs out as a molten stream, and then the molder can shape his metal as he desires. He can divert the molten stream into various channels and make all kinds of things. Well, as I have indicated, we must be made liquid, and that is the great work of the Holy Spirit—to break up all that is hard in these natures of ours, to make us more liquid so that He can mold us and shape us into the image of the Lord. We are too hard for God to use. We lack love and sympathy. There is no heart-feeling for others. But in the fiery furnace of the Holy Spirit, hardness is changed into a molten stream, and we are molded as the Spirit of God desires.

FIRE PURIFIES

> *He shall sit as a refiner and purifier of silver.*
>
> (Malachi 3:3)

> *That the trial of your faith, being much more precious than of gold that perisheth, though it be tried with fire.*
>
> (1 Peter 1:7)

How does the Holy Spirit purify? He purifies by separation. That is how the refiner purifies his metal. In Malachi 3, the refiner is sitting there before the crucible and within such, there is the metal, the precious silver. How does the refiner know that his metal is ready for him to use? Well, he sits there; he tempers the fire; and then as the hard silver is made liquid, the fire operates, and the dross gradually comes to the surface, he keeps on separating the dross from the silver, skimming the surface as the dross is forced out of the metal through the action of the fire. He skims the surface, removes the dross, and when ultimately he sees his face reflected in the molten metal, he knows that it is ready. The Holy Spirit sits alongside the crucible of your life and mine, and as the fire, He keeps on separating the dross from the metal, and He will keep on with that holy work of His until He can see the face of the Lord He loves to magnify and glorify. Fire purifies.

Take the illustration of the great plague in London. In 1665 they walked through the streets and cried, "Bring out your dead; bring out your dead." And through the plague, multitudes died. The plague of 1665 was followed by the great fire of 1666, and as the result of that great fire, something happened. The whole city was purged of the dreaded disease. But something else happened. The fire not only destroyed germs bringing death to myriads, but it penetrated the soil. It warmed the soil and after a while, unknown flowers sprang up from long, deeply buried seeds. The warming of the soil made possible the wonderful fertility of the seeds.

So also is the great work of the Holy Spirit. There are those who have within them the long buried seeds of divine truth, and then the Holy Spirit operates, and as the Spirit of fire, He destroys the plague of sin. Then He penetrates and warms the soil, thereby causing the life to fructify and bear fruit to the glory of God. And so we sing,

Burn, burn, O love within my heart;
Burn fiercely night and day,

Till all the dross of earthly loves
Is burned and burned away.[8]

8. Frederick W. Faber, "O Jesus, Jesus," unknown date.

CHAPTER EIGHT:

THE HOLY SPIRIT IN 2 CORINTHIANS 3

In this chapter, we hope to show how to analyze and use these teachings of the Holy Spirit, the heritage of the saints, as messages to the saints. Begin by taking a chapter from the Bible, and trace all the references to the Holy Spirit in that chapter, and then set the references in order. If you begin with a very simple chapter, like the one we have before us, then you can take a more difficult chapter, and, after you have mastered the principle in respect to a chapter, commence using it to study a book. I would suggest that you take the epistle to the Ephesians; read it through very carefully; and then write down on a piece of paper all the verses in that epistle related to the Holy Spirit. Then have a very fitting word on each of the references. You will find a good many aspects of the work of the Spirit emphasized in the epistle to the Ephesians. And when you have mastered a chapter and a book, you can come to a series of books. You could get a message or two on "The Holy Spirit in the Gospels" and then a message or two on "The Holy Spirit in the Acts of the Apostles" and another message or two on "The Holy Spirit in the Epistles" and then, "The Holy Spirit in the Revelation." The same applies to the Old Testament.

As an example of studying "The Holy Spirit in a Chapter," we take 2 Corinthians 3. Now, in this chapter you have four references to the Holy Spirit: in the third verse: (and you must read the three verses together in order to discover the connection in the first three verses):

> *Do we begin again to commend ourselves? or need we, as some others, epistles of commendation to you, or letters of commendation from you? Ye are our epistle written in our hearts, known and read of all men: Forasmuch as ye are manifestly declared to be the epistle of Christ ministered by us, written not with ink, but with the Spirit of the living God; not in tables of stone, but in fleshy tables of the heart.* (Verses 1–3)

And then in verse 6:

> *Who also hath made us able ministers of the new testament; not of the letter, but of the spirit: for the letter killeth, but the spirit giveth life.*

And then in verses 17 and 18:

> *Now the Lord is that Spirit: and where the Spirit of the Lord is, there is liberty. But we all, with open face beholding*

as in a glass the glory of the Lord, are changed into the same image from glory to glory, even as by the Spirit of the Lord.

There you have the four distinct references to the Holy Spirit in this chapter. You will see as you meditate upon these four passages that there is perfect order in the arrangement of the references. First of all is a reference to letters or epistles not written with ink but with the Spirit of the Living God. Then we find that the Holy Spirit is the Author of life. Having life, we pass on to know what liberty is. The other work of the Holy Spirit in the life of one who enjoys the liberty of the Spirit, who knows all about the life of the Spirit, who has been made a letter or an epistle of Christ, is likeness to the Lord Jesus. Let us now examine these verses.

VERSE 3: THE LETTER

You will see, in 2 Corinthians 3:3, that the apostle is saying, "*Ye are manifestly declared to be the epistle of Christ.*" In the first verse he is speaking about letters. "*Do we begin again to commend ourselves? Or need we, as some others, epistles of commendation to you, or letters of commendation from you?*" Then he goes on, "*Ye are our epistle written in our hearts, known and read of all men.*" Then he makes the application, "*Forasmuch as ye are manifestly declared to be the epistle of Christ ministered by us, written not with ink but with the Spirit of the living God; not in tables of stone, but in fleshy tables of the heart.*"

Here you have a very arresting simile. Paul is telling these Corinthians that they form the epistle or the letter of Christ, and that they form the only letter of commendation he needs, and that as a letter, they were written not in ink but with the Spirit of the living God. Now, how do you write a letter? Well, you write a letter with your fingers. If you have no fingers upon your hand, then it is not easy to write a letter, unless you can put the pen between your toes and write in that way. We have seen people who are armless writing letters with their toes. But ordinarily, we write a letter with our fingers.

If you look to the reference in Luke 11:20, you will find that our Lord speaks about the Holy Spirit as the finger of God. "*The finger of God.*" No matter how good and efficient the pen, it is not able to write a letter by itself. It is only as the pen is in the fingers of a living person that it can write. So here is the apostle saying that those Corinthian believers form his letter of commendation, and that they were written not in ink but with the Spirit of the living God. He is the finger and He wrote the letter. He made possible the life commending the Lord Jesus.

In your message, you could concentrate on this simile and show something of the points of contrast and comparison with an ordinary letter. Keep in mind this thought, however, that the letter is written by the Spirit of the living God; that He is the Finger penning the letter in you; that Christ-likeness in our lives is made possible through the direct operation of the Spirit of God.

VERSE 6: THE LIFE

In 2 Corinthians 3:6, He is referred to as the Spirit giving life. "*Who also hath made us able ministers of the New Testament; not of the letter, but of the spirit; for the letter killeth, but the spirit giveth life.*"

"*The spirit giveth life.*" Of course, here in the narrative, Paul is referring to the power pulsating through the Word. It is possible to be correct in our declaration of the Word and yet cold.

"The letter killeth, but the spirit giveth life." And so here the direct interpretation is the power pulsating through the Word. And in the declaration of the truth it is incumbent upon us to give the direct interpretation first of all, and then to make any application the Spirit of God may lead us to make.

Taking this phrase, *"the spirit giveth life,"* we go back to the third verse only to find where the Spirit receives His life from. He is referred to, as you can see, as the Spirit of the living God. So as the Spirit of the *living* God, He has power to give *life*. You already know how, in Romans 8:2, He is referred to as the Spirit of life. *"For the law of the Spirit of life in Christ Jesus hath made me free from the law of sin and death."* The Spirit of life—the Spirit of the living God. And as such He is able to give, to impart life.

You could work out a very suggestive outline on this very verse, something like "The Holy Spirit as the Author of Life." Show that He is the Author of natural life, of physical life, of spiritual life. You would take references in the Old Testament by the aid of your concordance. Begin with Genesis 1:2, the Spirit of God brooding over that chaotic condition of things and bringing order out of chaos and life out of death. Follow out the thought that He is responsible for natural life. Then you come to show that He is the Author of physical life, and if you wanted a fitting narrative, you could take Ezekiel 37. The valley of dry bones; how could they live? The wind from the four corners of the earth breathed upon them. And we know that wind is the simile of the ministry of the Holy Spirit, for He is able to raise up *"an exceeding great army"* (verse 10). Then, of course, you could use Romans 8:11, where the apostle tells us that the Holy Spirit has the power to quicken even the mortal body. So He is the Author of natural life; He is the Author of physical life; and He is the Author of spiritual life. Under this last aspect you could use John 3:5–7, where our Lord, speaking to Nicodemus, emphasizes this truth: that Nicodemus could only live spiritually as he was wrought upon by the Holy Spirit.

This phrase, *"The Spirit giveth life"* has been a great help to me in the ministry. In the earlier days of my ministry, when I was associated with evangelistic work, I was very keen on securing results, and used to resort to all kinds of methods to bring men and women to make some public decision for Christ. But with the passing years I have come to rely more upon the Holy Spirit than upon methods. I feel that so often in evangelistic work, we take this sacred task out of the hands of the Holy Spirit. Our solemn obligation, brethren, is to live in touch with the Holy Spirit, and to preach the Word that He presses in upon our mind and leave the results with him. You remember how we read in the book of Acts that while Peter preached the Word, the Holy Spirit fell upon the people. *"The Spirit giveth life."* Sometimes I hear evangelists who are over-enthusiastic; they plead and plead. They plead as if regeneration depended upon their pleading. *"The Spirit giveth life." "The wind bloweth where it listeth, and thou hearest the sound thereof, but canst not tell whence it cometh, and whither it goeth; so is every one that is born of the Spirit"* (John 3:8). And there will never be a lack of spiritual births in evangelistic campaigns if we live in the spirit of this sixth verse—*"The Spirit giveth life."*

VERSE 17: THE LIBERTY

Here we come to a verse we touched upon in a previous study—2 Corinthians 3:17, *"Now the Lord is that Spirit, and where the Spirit of the Lord is, there is liberty."* A wonderful truth. The Revised Standard Version expresses the opening phrase this way: *"Now the Lord is the Spirit."* The early church experienced remarkable liberty because she recognized continually the lordship of the Spirit. In Psalm 51:12, where the psalmist is found saying, *"Uphold me with thy free spirit."* The margin has it, "the Spirit of liberty," and His liberty is always experienced where His lordship is recognized. We need to get back to the lordship of the Spirit in church life and work. We do not have liberty today. We do not have the liberty of the Spirit in the organized church because we do not recognize the lordship of the Spirit.

By the way, there are three mediums of freedom or liberty that would make a very interesting Bible reading. First of all, there is the one in John 8:32, where Jesus says, *"And ye shall know the truth, and the truth shall make you free."* So the Word of God frees, and then the Son of God frees. *"If the Son therefore shall make ye free, ye shall be free indeed."* And here you have the Spirit of God. *"Where the Spirit of the Lord is, there is liberty"* (2 Corinthians 3:17). There you have a Trinity in unity. Through the Word of God and Son of God and the Spirit of God, we can enjoy full liberty.

In the context, liberty is associated with the law, freedom from the law—living no longer under the law, emphasized by Moses—but being *in* lawed to Jesus Christ. How do you think this liberty operates? Here again I will suggest to you a line that you can work out some week for a sermon on the Lord's Day. Show how the Holy Spirit is responsible for liberty in mind, liberty in life, liberty in prayer, liberty in worship, and liberty in service. Oh, what wonderful assemblies we would have if only we could experience the lordship of the Spirit in these particular ways.

1. The Holy Spirit is responsible for liberty in *mind*. It is He who delivers the mind; and it is a glad day in the experience of a

person when the Holy Spirit works upon the mind and liberates it from all ignorance, error, prejudice, and jealousy. So often we fail to give the Holy Spirit the liberty He wants with the mind. It may be that we have been brought up in a certain theological school and we have accepted the teachings emphasized by that school. Thus, when we come to a particular passage of the Word of God, we bring to it the particular interpretations or the prejudices of the school in question and do not give the Holy Spirit the liberty He desires in the mind.

Now, possibly you have been fighting against some particular truth on which emphasis has been laid. What you have heard from this platform from one speaker and another has seemed to contradict what you have been taught in a certain theological school. Give the Holy Spirit the liberty He wants in your mind. Freedom in the mind makes for wonderful freedom in the life.

2. He is responsible for liberty in *life*. It is sadly possible for us to have life and yet not to know what it is to have constant liberty. Lazarus had life, but he did not have liberty when he came forth from the grave. He had all the life it was possible for him to possess, but he did not have liberty, seeing he was bound hand and foot with grave clothes. Jesus had to say, *"Loose him, and let him go"* (John 11:44); and by so doing, Lazarus came to have liberty as well as life. Have you full liberty in life? It may be that you are not making very much progress because of secret sympathy with some form of sin. Appetites of the flesh impede your progress. The Holy Spirit waits to give you liberty in life. He is the *Holy* Spirit, and He can never bless these lives of ours if we entertain anything contrary to His holy mind and will.

3. He is responsible for liberty in *prayer*. I think we ought to emphasize this in our churches. There is a vast difference between saying prayers and praying. There are a good many

people who never get away from the repetition of worn-out phrases. Every time they pray they have the same thing to say, and one grows tired of listening to them in a prayer meeting. There are other people, who, when retiring to rest, repeat the same old prayer they have repeated for years. Well, you can teach a parrot to say a prayer. There is such a thing, however, as prayer in the Holy Spirit—praying in the Spirit. And the Holy Spirit is the inspirer of such effective prayer.

How do we have liberty in prayer? May we all be delivered from our bondage in this part of our liberty. There are those who can stand up and repeat a well-ordered prayer—a prayer they learned from the *Prayer Book*. I have nothing to say about some of those marvelous prayers that we have in the *Prayer Book of the Church of England*. But when they come to a prayer meeting they cannot express themselves freely; they are frozen stiff. They stumble over a few sentences, simply because they do not know what it is to have the Holy Spirit as the Spirit of liberty in their prayer life. Now, let us trust the Holy Spirit to make us efficient in this respect. Prayer is a gift that increases with its use. And the more we depend upon the Spirit in our prayer life, the more will that prayer life become active and powerful; and depending upon the Spirit, we shall reap enrichment in our intercessory prayers.

4. He is responsible for liberty in *worship*. You will agree with me when I say that we need the liberty of the Holy Spirit in the worship of the church of God today. There will never be any bondage, neither will worship be cold, formal, and mechanical if the lordship of the Holy Spirit is recognized. There will be no restraint where the Spirit of God is in full control of an assembly. Atmosphere will be tense with His presence and power, and the worshippers will leave realizing that they have gazed into

the face of the eternal One. They will also carry away with them something of the fragrance of the sanctuary in which they have worshipped.

Before Russia was brought under the power of the Soviet government, there was a church in Moscow where they used a certain kind of incense. It had a remarkable fragrance, and as it was burned, the entire sanctuary became permeated with the odor of that particular incense; and the people carried away with them the incense of the sanctuary, and others could detect immediately where these people had worshipped. They were known by the fragrance of the sanctuary. And if we know what it is to have liberty in worship, then we carry away with us the fragrance of the house of God.

5. Then there will come liberty in *service*, and we certainly need this aspect of the Spirit's ministry. We need the Spirit of liberty. There is the tendency to serve God simply because we have to. This is one thing that we have to guard against in ministry. You see, we are accustomed to these holy things. This is our particular work. God has made it possible for us to preach and teach the Word. And it is sadly possible just to come to this task because we have to. Brethren, we must never look upon ourselves as waiters merely; that is, coming to the Word and dividing it up, and then, when we have it nicely arranged, just to convey it to the hungry people who are before us. We must be guests at the table as well as waiters. We must know what it is to be fed ourselves before we can feed others. And unless I have liberty in my service and know what it is to be free, there will be a sense of bondage when I come to minister the Word. Liberty in service! And when there is liberty in service, there is no reliance upon self-made plans. We are open to the suggestions of the Holy Spirit and we move along as He may dictate.

VERSE 18: THE LIKENESS

Then the Holy Spirit is associated with likeness. Second Corinthians 3:18 says, *"But we all, with open face beholding as in a glass the glory of the Lord, are changed into the same image from glory to glory, even as the Spirit of the Lord."* Here we have a very interesting application. The word image there means likeness. Lordship of the Spirit over the life results in liberty in life, and where the liberty of the Spirit is enjoyed, there comes likeness to Christ. Now the great passion of the Holy Spirit is to make us like Jesus. You must not think that because we are dwelling upon the Holy Spirit in these days that we are blind to the fact that the Lord Jesus must be preeminent in all things. The more you study the Holy Spirit, the more you will strive to find out what the Bible has to say about the Lord Jesus. As you study the words of Jesus, He sends you to the Holy Spirit, and the Holy Spirit sends you to Jesus. And the more you discover about the Spirit, the more will He lead you to exalt Jesus in your ministry. These two are One.

The great passion, then, of the Holy Spirit is to make us like Jesus. It was the Holy Spirit who operated to make Jesus like God, in respect to the revelation of God among men. And now in this dispensation, it is the Holy Spirit who strives to make us like Jesus, and, as you can see, it is a daily transformation. How does the Holy Spirit make possible this likeness? How do we take on the image of the Lord? Well, in these ways: in the hatred of sin, in our Lord's loving disposition, in His prayerful dependence upon His Father, in His passion for Scripture, in His submission to the will of God. The Holy Spirit makes these possible in our lives. A word or two regarding each of them:

1. He makes us like the Lord Jesus in that He creates within our hearts the same hatred for sin that burned in the heart of

the Lord Jesus. You see He is the "Holy" Spirit, and, as the Holy Spirit, His glad work in your heart and mind is to transform us into the likeness of the Lord in this respect, to make us holy even as Jesus is holy. And the Holy Spirit dwelling within takes away the love of sinning.

2. Then it is He who makes possible the loving disposition and attractive winsomeness that characterized the life of the Lord Jesus. It has been truly said that if we would win some, we must be winsome. We can only win some, as Jesus won disciples, when we know something of the winsomeness of Jesus.

In the previous chapter we were exhorted to have dignity, courtesy, humility, and other necessary traits. We are not left to ourselves to produce these traits. We can never manufacture them, but as we submit to the Holy Spirit, He makes us God's gentlemen. It is He who produces the loving disposition and the attractive winsomeness Jesus possessed. This is not mere imitation. We have a hymn that has a phrase in it about being like Jesus, and there are those who try to imitate Jesus. But that is not the principle the New Testament enunciates. We are not to try and imitate the Lord Jesus; we must be submissive to the Holy Spirit and allow Him to transform us into likeness to Christ, for the work of the Spirit is to continue the life of Jesus in your life and mine. He makes possible this prayerful dependence upon the Father. Our Lord lived a life of prayerfulness. At every turn of the way, you find Him depending upon the Father.

That is a very interesting study, "The Prayer Life of our Lord." We said that the Holy Spirit inspires prayer. That is made clear in Romans 8:26, "*We know not what we should pray for as we ought, but the Spirit itself maketh intercession for us with groanings which cannot be uttered.*" As He sustained Jesus in His prayer life, as He inspired Jesus to pray, so He makes possible in our ministry this prayerful dependence upon the Father.

3. He makes possible our passion for the Word of God. The Old Testament, the only Bible Jesus had, was stored in His heart. There was the source of His strength—His stay amid all the testing of His life. He quoted the Word of God in the wilderness and defeated the devil by it. And right through His ministry, you find Him quoting the Word of God. When He came to die, the Word of God was still upon His lips. Why did Jesus use the Word of God so continuously? Well, you discover why if you turn to Ephesians 6:17, *"And take the helmet of salvation, and the sword of the Spirit, which is the word of God."* The Word of God is the sword of the Spirit. The Holy Spirit enabled our Lord so to repeat the Word that the repetition of the Word made for victory. And the Holy Spirit makes us like Jesus by the creation of a passion for the Word of God.

4. Then, in the last place, the Spirit of God transforms us into likeness of Jesus in that He makes possible submission to the divine will. When Jesus left heaven, in respect to His humanity, He died to sin, in that He became dependent upon the Father, submissive to the Father. That is why we find Him saying in Gethsemane, *"Not my will, but thine, be done"* (Luke 22:42). Left to ourselves, there are many things we cannot do when we are brought to a crisis. But what may be impossible to the flesh is blessedly possible as we allow the Holy Spirit to have His way. For He makes possible the same submission to the divine will.

Thus, we have tried to analyze the teaching of this chapter and if you take these principles, they will help you as you give yourself to the study of another chapter or book of the Bible.

The Holy Spirit is responsible for the transformation of the life. He fashions us into the letter or the epistle of Christ. He is the Author of life. He is the Author of liberty. It is He who transforms us into the likeness of Christ.

Allow one illustration in closing. In St. Peter's, Cologne, there are two pictures of the Crucifixion of Peter that stand side by side, and the existence of these two pictures is explained in this way: In the beginning of the nineteenth century, when Napoleon came and ransacked the city, he robbed St. Peter's of one of those two pictures—the original—and took it away. While the first picture was away from the city, the artist, in the absence of the original, painted another picture. In time the original picture was restored, and the two were placed side by side. Experts now say that there is so little difference between the two pictures you cannot tell which is the original. In the absence of the original, the artist painted another picture of Peter. Now, that is the glorious work of the Spirit. The Original is absent. Jesus is in heaven. But the Holy Spirit is here, and He is the Master Artist, and in the absence of the Original, He is painting the likeness of Jesus upon the unworthy canvas of your life and mine. May we be worthy copies of the Original—conformed to His likeness!

ABOUT THE AUTHOR

When Dr. Herbert Lockyer (1886–1984) was first deciding on a career, he considered becoming an actor. Tall and well-spoken, he seemed a natural for the theater. But the Lord had something better in mind. Instead of the stage, God called Herbert to the pulpit, where, as a pastor, a Bible teacher, and the author of more than fifty books, he touched the hearts and lives of millions of people.

Dr. Lockyer held pastorates in Scotland and England for twenty-five years. As pastor of Leeds Road Baptist Church in Bradford, England, he became a leader in the Keswick Higher Life Movement, which emphasized the significance of living in the fullness of the Holy Spirit. This led to an invitation to speak at the Moody Bible Institute's fiftieth anniversary in 1936. His warm reception at that event led to his ministry in the United States. He received honorary degrees from both the Northwestern Evangelical Seminary and the International Academy in London.

In 1955, he returned to England, where he lived for many years. He then returned to the United States, where he spent the final years of his life in Colorado Springs, Colorado, with his son, the Rev. Herbert Lockyer Jr., a Presbyterian minister who eventually became his editor.